Magic, Myth, and Merrymaking:

13 Days of Yuletide the Old Mermaids Way

Also by Kim Antieau

Old Mermaids Books
The Blue Tail • Church of the Old Mermaids
The First Book of Old Mermaids Tales • The Fish Wife
An Old Mermaid Journal • The Old Mermaids Book of Days and Nights
The Old Mermaids Book of Days and Nights: A Year and a Day Journal
The Old Mermaids Mystery School • The Old Mermaids Oracle
The Old Mermaids Wisdom Cards

Other Novels
Broken Moon • Butch • Coyote Cowgirl • Deathmark
The Desert Siren • Her Frozen Wild • The Gaia Websters
Jewelweed Station • The Jigsaw Woman • Killing Beauty
Mercy, Unbound • The Monster's Daughter • Queendom: Feast of the Saints •
The Rift • Ruby's Imagine • Swans in Winter • Whackadoodle Times
Whackadoodle Times Two • Whackadoodle Times Three
Whackadoodle Times Galore

Other Nonfiction
Answering the Creative Call • Certified: Learning to Repair Myself and the World in the Emerald City • Counting on Wildflowers: An Entanglement MommaEarth Goddess Runes • The Salmon Mysteries: a Reimagining of the Eleusinian Mysteries • Under the Tucson Moon: Nine Winters in the Sonoran Desert

MAGIC, MYTH, AND MERRYMAKING

13 Days of Yuletide the Old Mermaids Way

Kim Antieau

Green Snake
PUBLISHING

Magic, Myth, and Merrymaking:
13 Days of Yuletide the Old Mermaids Way
by Kim Antieau

Copyright © 2021 by Kim Antieau

All rights reserved.
No part of this book may be reproduced without written permission of the author.

ISBN: 978-1-949644-63-0

Photos by Annie Spratt, Corina Andrisca, Satheesh Sankaran, Leone Venter, Lydia Matzal, Miro Slava, and Kim Antieau.

Cover image by Joanna Kosinska.

Thanks to Nancy Milosevic.

Published by Green Snake Publishing
www.greensnakepublishing.com

Contents

Introduction: Magic, Myth, and Merrymaking • 7

Day One: Night of the Mother • 17
Grand Mother Yemaya Mermaid

Day Two: Solstice • 41
Sister DeeDee Lightful Mermaid

Day Three: Day of the Hummingbird • 71
Sister Lyra Musica Mermaid

Day Four: Day of the Bean • 91
Sister Ruby Rosarita Mermaid

Day Five: Day of the Deer • 111
Sister Laughs A Lot Mermaid

Day Six: Day of the Sun • 139
Sister Sophia Mermaid

Day Seven: Day of the Bear • 157
Sister Ursula Divine Mermaid

Day Eight: Day of the Song • *179*
   Sister Bridget Mermaid

Day Nine: Day of the Saguaro • *195*
   Sister Shelia Na Giggles Mermaid

Day Ten: Day of the Queen of the Night • *213*
   Sister Magdelene Mermaid

Day Eleven: Day of the Owl • *233*
   Sister Bea Wilder Mermaid

Day Twelve: Day of the Dragonfly • *253*
   Sister Faye Mermaid

Day Thirteen: Day of the Desert Tortoise • *275*
   Mother Star Stupendous Mermaid

About the Author • *301*

Introduction
Magic, Myth, and Merrymaking

When I was a child, I loved the winter holidays. All the rituals seemed laden with mystery, joy, and magic. On Christmas Eve, we woke up in the middle of the night to sleepily dress for midnight mass while *A Christmas Carol* played on our tiny black and white TV in the living room.

After church, we drove to my grandmother's house down the road—usually on treacherous snowy roads—where our big Catholic family gathered to feast and open presents. Grandma always had a gift under the tree for all her grandkids, which was amazing in itself since there were 15 or 20 of us, depending upon who was in town.

At home again, my four sisters and I would sleep upstairs in our beds for a few hours. When it was still dark out, we would run quietly downstairs to discover a couple dozen presents Santa and his elves had left under the tree for us.

That time when my sisters and I lay on the wooden floor or on the couch in the living room, our faces lit only by the Christmas tree lights as we gazed at the gifts under the tree—that time before we knew what was inside each box, before we noticed that Santa had signed the cards on the gifts in Mom and Dad's handwriting—was filled with such delicious mystery and potential for magic.

As the years went by, the holidays became less fun, often fraught with family tensions and a busy-ness that was exhausting. It wasn't until I discovered that most Christmas traditions had Pagan roots that it became interesting to me again.

Then the Old Mermaids came into my life. When they left the Old Sea and washed ashore onto the New Desert, they learned the rituals and ceremonies of the Old Neighbors and combined them with their own way of being in the world. Soon the whole community was celebrating the Old Mermaids Way which meant the days and nights between Solstice and New Year's Day were filled with magic, mystery, and merrymaking again.

Who Are the Old Mermaids?

The Old Mermaids began as characters in my novel *Church of the Old Mermaids.* In the book, their lives in the Old Sea ended when they washed ashore onto the New Desert where they "exchanged their finware for skinware." They had to learn not only how to survive but how to thrive in this new land.

When the Old Mermaids left the Old Sea and came to the New Desert, the ways they had lived and celebrated in the Old Sea didn't fit any longer. So they listened to the land and their human neighbors, and they figured out how to live and celebrate every day as best they could, including during the holidays. In this book, you will find some of the magical ways the Old Mermaids celebrated Winter Solstice and the return of the light.

I wrote *Church of the Old Mermaids* while staying at a writing retreat in the Sonoran Desert. The setting for the novel was very much like where we stayed. In fact, we renamed the retreat the Old Mermaids Sanctuary.

About 15 years after we started coming to the retreat, the place came up for sale, and we were able to buy it. We now live on the Old Mermaids Sanctuary.

For myself and my readers, over time, the 13 Old Mermaids have become more than just characters in a book. I often ask myself, "What would the Old Mermaids do?" They have troubles, yet they try to spread beauty in the world, in all the meanings of that word.

The Old Mermaids are realists, they don't hide their heads in the sand, they help out their community, and they are dreamers, magic-makers, artists, carpenters, seamstresses, faeries, and more. They don't judge, and they don't adhere to dogma. They look to Nature for most answers to most questions.

What is Winter Solstice?

The word solstice comes from the Latin *sol* (sun) and *sistere* (to stand still). At this time of year, because of where the Earth is in its orbit, the Sun appears—from Earth's viewpoint—to stand still or pause before continuing. In the northern hemisphere, (around) Winter Solstice is the longest night of the year, and (around) Summer Solstice is the longest day of the year. After Winter Solstice, the days grow longer: The light has returned!

This astronomical event was noted and celebrated long before organized religion. During the yuletide season, our ancestors celebrated and prepared themselves spiritually and physically to get through the winter. For them, being in connection with Nature and their ancestors was part of their every day lives. Celebrations and rituals helped keep these connections strong and vibrant.

The folklore, rituals, and ceremonies associated with Winter Solstice are vast, varied, and deep. For some, this longest night of the year marked the beginning of a period of going inward. The harvest was in. It was cold and most often snowy outside, so people stayed indoors telling tales, keeping warm, and watching for signs of their ancestors.

For others, it was a time of celebration, of gathering with family and friends; it was a time for dancing, feasting, and merrymaking. In Scotland, for instance, the 12 days of Yuletide were called the "daft days."

Many of our modern Christmas traditions began long ago. Santa Claus seems to have almost endless beginnings and meanings. He probably was an ancient Pagan god or an arctic shaman. Perhaps his eight reindeer symbolize the eight major sabbats of the traditional Pagan year. (Can you figure out which reindeer goes with which sabbat?)

For some European Pagans, mistletoe was the "golden bough" which helped gain entrance to the underworld. According to Barbara Walker, to the Nordic Pagans, "mistletoe represented the death of the savior god Balder, son of Odin, whose second coming was expected after doomsday."

The Irish call mistletoe *drualas,* which means "Druid's herb." It was considered an all-heal plant. Apparently the Druids believed the white berries were drops of the Oak God's semen. When they cut the mistletoe from the trees, they were essentially castrating the Oak God. The plant was associated with fertility, so newly married couples kissed beneath it to ensure their fertility.

And of course, the pine tree—the evergreen tree—symbolizes everlasting life. What better symbol during the long dark days and nights of winter?

What Are the 13 Days of Yuletide the Old Mermaids Way?

This book is about looking at the yuletide season in another way, especially if you have been feeling burned out, alone, or disconnected during the holidays. The Old Mermaids and their way of being can bring us home to ourselves.

In this book, you will find practices, recipes, activities, and bits of Old Em magic to help you celebrate the days and nights from December 20th to January 1st.

Also, for the first time, I write about how the Old Mermaids got their names. As a bonus, writer Mario Milosevic has written a special poem for each day.

Don't feel obligated to do all the practices within—or any of them, actually. This book isn't about being busy. It is about building a bridge to the next year, a year that we hope will bring us good health, joy, love, and prosperity. Each of these 13 days will be building blocks for that bridge, whether you do the practices or not. Reading this kind of material can be like a transmission, and your highest self will take it from there.

I tried to make the practices as simple as possible. I like simple. You can do them alone or with other people. Use whatever materials you have right on hand. The Old Mermaids are masters of improvisation, and you can be, too. Nothing I say or instruct here is set in stone. You get to use your imagination and change it however you like.

By the way, some years Winter Solstice is on December 22. In those years, just read the December 22 chapter on December 21 and the Solstice chapter on December 22.

The Old Mermaids come from all over the world, they have a variety of skin colors and ethnicities, yet they are their own culture with their own set of beliefs, rituals, and practices. However, my heritage is mostly Western European. I have lived on lands that are within the United States all my life. Most of the stories and references I make here will be based on Northern and Western European traditions. This isn't because I don't respect and honor other cultures: It is because I do.

For the most part, I won't suggest practices based on spiritualities and religions that aren't part of my culture unless it is an activity that is practiced in many cultures. In those cases, we don't always know where the practices began. For instance, putting out prayer flags is a tradition in Tibet that has spread worldwide, and it may have started with the shamanic Bön people. But other people from other cultures have tied strips of cloth to trees, too, hoping their desires are carried to their ancestors or any divine being who can help make those wishes come true. I am comfortable sharing those kinds of practices.

Have fun!

Blessed sea,

Kim Antieau

Day One
Night of the Mothers

December 20

Ahhh. The day and night before Solstice was sometimes called Mother Night. The Old Neighbors who lived near the Old Mermaids Sanctuary certainly made this night a festival, one with lots of good things to eat. You get to choose. Maybe too much is going on around you this time of year, and it's squeezing the magic out of everything. So you'll want to find some quiet moments for yourself. Or perhaps it is feeling too quiet this year. In that case, maybe you want to make yourself a special meal—or order one in?

One night a year isn't enough to honor mothers and creation, but it is a start. Mother Night was celebrated by Anglo-Saxon people on the night before Christmas and by other Pagans on or before Solstice. It is a recognition that the creative forces in the world are responsible for all life. As the Wheel of the Year turns toward the light, we turn away from darkness, introspection, and destruction and look forward to light and life starting again.

Dreams

Pay attention to your dreams during this time. Don't worry if you don't dream a lot. Think about putting paper and pen by your bed so you can write down dreams in the middle of the night or when you first awaken in the morning. You might find messages from your ancestors or your "higher" self in these dreams.

Consider employing what I call "daydreaming." This is a method I use to go back into a dream and explore it. It can also be used if you haven't had a dream at all. For instance if I'm writing about deer in the 13 Days of Yuletide, I might encourage you to "daydream" about a deer. To do this, close your eyes, and imagine that you come across a deer during your day. Is the deer on a path you are walking? Is it in the road in front of your car? Is it flying through the sky? Is it on the cover of a book?

What would happen next? What would happen if the deer turned to you and began to talk? What would it say to you? See if you can carry on a conversation with it. Or maybe you follow the deer and it takes you to a place where a message or symbol awaits you.

This method is especially helpful if you're having a dream drought. This helps you take some control over your dreaming while still letting your subconscious or imagination create the dream. Sometimes this kind of daydreaming takes practice. Don't worry: Just practice.

What did you dream last night? Were there any messages from the Ancestors or your higher self? Look for messages from the female side of your family. Write about all of this if you like.

Ground and Center

Healing Roots Meditation

If you already have a way of grounding and centering yourself first thing each morning, you can go ahead and use your own method, of course.

If you don't have your own method or you want to try something new, here is one of the ways the Old Mermaids learned to ground and center when they washed ashore on the New Desert.

Imagine roots growing down from the bottoms of your feet and into the ground. They grow down, down, down, travelling through dirt and rock. Your roots are strong, and they make it all the way to the center of the Earth, to the heart of the Earth.

Let the tips of your roots dip into the molten center of the Earth: They are not singed. Instead, healing energy from the Earth goes up your roots, up, up, up, until this healing energy reaches the bottom of your feet. The energy fills your feet, your legs, your abdomen, your spine, your lungs, your heart, your head: It fills your entire body. You may even want to raise your hands to the sky as the healing energy fills your body. Then let the healing energy naturally drain away as your arms drop down to the side of your body again, leaving you energized and healed. As the healing energy drains, your roots move back up into the bottoms of your feet. There! Now you are grounded and centered.

Look for Guides and Signs

As you awaken in the morning during this time, be on the lookout for yuletide guides. Did you dream of a certain plant or animal? If so, consider it as your guide for the day. If not, go outside. Does something unusual catch your eye? Is a particular bird singing louder than usual? Is there a line of ants crossing your path? Has the oleander bush outside your door suddenly blossomed? If so, do a quick (or long) meditation and ask yourself and the spirit of this creature or plant if they will act as your guide either for this day or for the 13 days. If the answer is no, just move along. Don't stress about it. Your guide may turn out to be a rock. Or a horse you see on the side of a van. If nothing "appears," don't worry about it. It just means it's not part of your process either for today or perhaps for the entire 13 days.

You can also look for signs. Robert Moss calls it "sidewalk tarot." As you are out walking, watch for something unusual. For instance, what if a live snake suddenly slithered out in front of you? It's winter time so that would be unusual. You could interpret this like you would a dream. What would seeing a snake in a dream mean to you? Don't look it up in a dream book or ask someone else. What is its significance to you? Could it mean "remember to be close to the Earth?" Is it telling you to "shed your skin" metaphorically? Snakes are associated with the goddess Athena. Does she have a message for you?

Again, don't stress about it. Go with what first comes to you because it is your interpretation that is important. The snake would have been there whether you were in the neighborhood or not. So why were *you* there? What would you mean to the snake if it was her dream? That's always fun to contemplate.

There aren't right or wrong answers. It's about you being connected to your environment.

Ceremony

This is the Night of the Mothers. It is a time to honor your maternal ancestors. If your mother and grandmother are alive, tell them how much they mean to you. Or tell an aunt. A sister. Honor the creative force in the world in whatever way you see fit. Honor yourself no matter your gender.

    Get a candle, candle holder, and matches. Then safely light the candle. If you don't have a candle just sit quietly in the dark. Envision a circle of safety around you. Call out to your maternal ancestors. Tell them you are grateful for all they did to survive. They are why you are here today. Imagine the generations of mothers, sisters, daughters that are represented within you. Be grateful for that which strengthens and nourishes you. Imagine all that doesn't serve you from your female ancestors released from your body. When that feels complete, put out the flame on the candle. Watch the smoke rising—or imagine it if it's too dark to see; imagine all that doesn't serve you disappearing as the smoke disappears. Thank your ancestors again. Open the circle. *May the circle be open but unbroken. Merry meet and merry part and merry meet again.*

Magic

Time to tidy! If cleaning your whole house or apartment feels exhausting, pick one room or one corner, and tidy it. Clean another corner or room each day of the 13.

Think of how great it will be to have a place for everything and everything in its place by the new year. Do it all with intention. Cleaning is magic. Think of the witch's broom. She is sweeping away more than dust. As you clean, release illness, poverty, and strife, and bring in good health, prosperity, and peace.

The Old Mermaids may or may not be faeries. Some say that

faeries don't like clutter. So if you want faery visitors, you know what to do.

Gift

Everyone in the orbit of the Old Mermaids is Gifted. It's a ceremony one usually goes through as a child, but one can be "gifted" at any age. The Old Mermaids say, "I gift you with enough to eat," "I gift you with laughter," or "I gift you with courage." Every day of these 13 Yuletide Days, the Old Mermaids will gift you. It is a gift you've had all along, and now you're reminded of it.

Today, they gift you with Mysteries of the Old Sea.

Old Mermaid Suggestion

"Laugh or weep, we swim in your tears."

—*Grand Mother Yemaya Mermaid*

Recipe for Morning Blessing Water

The Old Mermaids' recipes are about magic and transformation whether food is involved or not. Here's a recipe to honor water.

Get a glass of water. Take it outside. Stand still and silent as you hold it. Be aware of the sounds and sights around you. Think about what it took to get that water into your kitchen. Imagine it flowing over mountain streams or through underground aquifers.

Feel your gratitude bubbling over. Give thanks. Take a sip of the water. Then pour a bit on the ground. Next either stay outside while drinking the water, or return inside and add it to your coffee, tea, or whatever else you are cooking.

Old Mermaid Tale

Jewels

When the Old Mermaids first washed up on the shores of the New Desert, they were bereft. Naturally. Their beloved Old Sea was gone, at least as far as they could see or hear or feel. Everyone and everything they had loved except each other, the Moon, Sun, Stars, and Earth were disappeared to them.

At first, it was like coming out of a dream for most of the 13 (even though the Old Ems didn't really dream like we do, at least not before they reached the New Desert). They felt groggy and foggy and not quite like themselves because, of course, they were no longer quite themselves. They had experienced and survived a terrible trauma. They would never be the same.

That first night—or was it the second?—darkness fell as the Old Mermaids huddled in the wash together, naked as mermaids who have lost their tails to legs would be coming straight from the Old Sea. Grand Mother Yemaya Mermaid worried about her sister mermaids. What could she do to comfort them? She could not tell them all was well because it was not. She could not tell them what steps they would take next because she had no idea. She knew Sisters Bridget and Faye Mermaid were listening to the World to try to hear what the Wind and the Wild had to tell them. She knew Sissy Maggie Mermaid would try to find something to love here. But right this moment, Grand Mother Yemaya Mermaid could think of nothing to do or not do.

As the night wore on, the darkness deepened.

"All I want to do is cry," Sister Lyra Musica Mermaid said. "But I'm afraid I will never stop."

Grand Mother Yemaya Mermaid said, "Nothing is forever."

Sister Lyra Musica Mermaid began to sob. Soon Sister Bea Wilder Mermaid was hiccuping with sorrow. And then Sister DeeDee Lightful Mermaid cried. The weeping went around to all the Old Ems. As they cried, the jewels they had pressed into the sides of the arroyo when they first washed ashore began to glow in the dark, one after another: gold, emerald green, maroon, silver, white, sun yellow, sky blue. It was a beautiful thing to behold.

The tears of the Old Mermaids streamed down their faces and fell into the dry wash. After a while, the Old Mermaids felt water on their new feet and thought for a moment that the Old Sea had returned. Alas, it was not to be. The wash was filling up with their tears. The Old Mermaids scrambled up out of the wash that was now a creek as the Sun came up. Several of the New Neighbors rushed toward them.

"Oh, what good luck you are," one of the women said as she took off her shawl and put it around one of the Old Mermaids. "This wash has been dry for a lifetime or more."

One by one the neighbors came from all around to see the New Creek and their new neighbors. They brought food and clothes for the Old Mermaids, and they all introduced themselves to each other.

Sister Magdelene Mermaid put on a long yellow sun dress and opened her arms to the day. "Look what the tears have brought us," she said.

"Indeed," Grand Mother Yemaya Mermaid said as she wrapped her hair up in a long purple scarf. She wiped away her last tears. "It is a good day."

And so their life in the New Desert began in earnest.

Poetry by Mario Milosevic

Homecoming

The ocean hugs the seabed
just as trees grip the ground.

Marine currents recognize
kinship with the restless wind.

No need for confinement to one sphere
when we are made for all realms.

Your roots are my roots
and home is imagination's way

of keeping all beings close
to the embrace of the world.

Action

What action can you take today? Honor the Old Sea or any waterway. You can donate money to an organization protecting waterways, or you could clean up an area near a waterway (a shoreline or beach). If you don't know your watershed, find out what it is. You can usually find out by looking it up online or phoning your city or water department.

And a Little Herstory

Yemaya is a great African goddess, mother of oceans and all that is within. In *Church of the Old Mermaids*, Grand Mother Yemaya Mermaid knows all the secrets of everything. In her book *Jambalaya*, Luisah Teish writes, "Yemaya-Olokun is the Mother of the Sea, the Great Water, the Womb of Creation. She is the Mother of Dreams, the Mother of Secrets . . . She is the mermaid, the full Moon; and intelligence beyond human comprehension."

Yes, indeed.

Day Two
Solstice

December 21

Winter Solstice is the shortest day and longest night of the year. On this day we acknowledge the darkness and celebrate that we have survived the longest night, we have survived the sometimes terrifying darkness of this year, and now we are reborn in light.

Today is a good day to remember our ancestors, human and non-human. We are made of stardust, so the Stars are also our ancestors. What we eat, drink, and breathe becomes part of our body, so everything we eat, drink, and breathe is part of our slate of Ancestors.

It is also a good time to look around more closely for the unseen. We know so little about our world. Yet most of our human ancestors believed in some kind of "little people," even when they weren't so little. In Japan, they were called the Yōsei. In Russia, most households host a Domovoy. In Australia, Mimis live in rock crevices.

Western Europe is apparently populated with a multitude of fairies, including the Tuatha Dé Danann: the folk of the goddess Danu. Some folklore suggests the Tuatha Dé Danann were the last race of gods in Ireland, eventually run off by the Celts. Now they live in Summerland or the Otherworld and work to balance and protect Nature. This is often the role of "fairies" no matter their name or culture.

If your ancestry is not Western European, you might want to investigate who your fairies might be and how to honor them. If your ancestry is Western European, we have been told by the Irish and others who may know about such things that fairies particularly like honey and milk. Consider putting out milk and honey for them, depending upon your situation.

You might even want to make a special altar for the fey, outside where most people won't see it or inside where you will see it enough to make certain it is always clean. Remember, fairies apparently love tiny and uncluttered spaces.

If the idea of fairies seems far-fetched to you, consider that the Mimis, fairies, and Domovoys are merely names that have been given to the natural forces that are with us all the time. Think about any place you have been, indoors or out. You are either attracted to a particular spot in these places or you are not. Why is that? Something in Nature is different there: It aligns with you in some way or it doesn't. But we don't know scientifically yet what the difference is.

I can feel what I call the heart of almost every place I visit. It's nothing supernatural or unscientific. It's just my name for the spot I'm most drawn to in an area or it's the place where energy (for lack of a better term) seems to eddy, and I want to go put my feet in that eddy.

We make offerings to the Ancestors, "fairies," or Nature not because we are superstitious. We do it out of respect of Nature and to remind ourselves that we are just a part of a big complicated whole that we don't completely understand yet.

Dreams

Pay attention to your dreams. Did you dream anything about darkness and light last night? Beginnings or endings? If you didn't, don't worry about it. You are incubating dreams even if you are not recalling them. I encourage you to write down whatever you are dreaming. See if there is some kind of pattern. Are you dreaming about any of the same things? For instance, a purse could show up in several dreams. If that happens, explore what a purse might mean to you. Was it lost in the dream or was it always with you, safe and secure?

Ground and Center

Use the Healing Roots Meditation from yesterday or your own practice to ground and center. The idea is to give yourself a moment of stillness and connection before you bounce into the day.

Look for Guides and Signs

Do you have a guide for these 13 days or are you looking for a new one each day? Either way, see if a guide has any messages for you. Perhaps the crow overhead caw-cawing is reminding you to wake up—or maybe she's just saying hello. Or that rock you pass every day suddenly looks like a sleeping rabbit. What does a rabbit mean to you? Is the world shapeshifting before you? Look at the clouds and contrails. Any messages? You're looking at the environment and interpreting it the way you would a dream or a painting to see what wisdom you can glean from it.

Ceremony

Dark Sun/Light Sun

You can do this with children or adults, depending upon who is in your household. We started creating these in our house about twenty years ago. I don't remember if I learned it from someone else or if we made it up. It's very simple. You'll need scissors, paper, glue or a stapler, single hole punch if you have one, crayons or colored pencils, and yarn, dental floss, or string. If you don't have crayons or colored pencils, I'm sure you have a black pen or pencil around the house, right? You can use dark and light construction paper if you have it, but I think actually drawing in the darkness and light on white paper helps us embody the spirit of this practice better.

Cut out several circles, whatever size you want, making sure the number divides by two. Or just cut two circles and see if you want to do more. First, color one circle black. Get it as dark as you can with whatever materials you have. Think of this past year and everything you would like to leave behind. In fact, you can write on the circle before you darken it. "Leaving behind fear. Leaving behind illness. Releasing poverty." Write whatever you want gone. Then color over these words until you cannot read them any longer.

Next, color a circle in light colors. Pick yellow or orange or something bright that represents light to you. While coloring it, think of what you want in the new year. Here again, you can write on the circle. "Bringing in good health. Prosperity all year round. World peace." Then color it. Since you're using a light bright color, you should still be able to see your wishes for the new year. Feel that lightness as you color. Imagine all good things coming your way.

If you're doing this with children, talk about the return of the Sun, and the celebration of light. We always made certain the kids didn't think darkness was bad. We talked about darkness being an incubator, like compost: darkness turning into nourishing soil. Darkness and light have a place in the world, and we celebrate both.

Next, staple or glue the circles together, colored sides out if you only colored one side. Punch a hole at the top of the circles and tie a loop of yarn or string or dental floss through it. Hang it on a doorknob with the dark sun facing out.

If you have limited supplies, you can color one side of a circle dark and the other side light instead of cutting out two circles each. In our experience this doesn't work quite as well because the dark colors tend to bleed through.

If you're doing more than one sun, you can change it up. On the light-colored circles, draw a wakeful face; on the dark-colored circles, draw a sleepy face. Hang these all over your house before you go to sleep, with the dark side facing out. In the morning, turn them all over so that the light sun is showing. This is great fun with children, but adults can enjoy this activity as well.

Magic

Solstice is a perfect time to do a little divination. Pull out your tarot cards and ask a question before doing a spread. For instance ask, "Help me truly see the light," or "How can I go forward and make this coming year a good one?"

If you don't own tarot cards, use any kind of divination tool you have on hand. You are essentially asking your higher self, your deep self, for advice. You are better able to give yourself advice and insight when you are interpreting a tarot reading or a dream.

If you don't have any kind of divination tool, make your own. You can make a quick and simple one by tearing 13 strips of paper. Then write the suggestion and name of the Old Mermaid on each strip. Fold them up and put them in a bowl. Ask your question, and then draw one strip out and see what the Old Mermaid suggests.

You can always "daydream" a meeting with that Old Mermaid and have a conversation with her. Whatever you do with the Old Mermaids, it is always magic.

Here are the names of the Old Mermaids with their suggestions all in one place:

Get the starfish outta your eyes, sister.
—*Sister Sheila Na Giggles Mermaid*

Step lightly. Dance hard. Eat your vegetables.
—*Sister DeeDee Lightful Mermaid*

Things change. Get over it.
—*Sister Bea Wilder Mermaid*

Fear has no sisters, but I have many.
—*Sister Lyra Musica Mermaid*

She who laughs a lot laughs a lot.
—*Sister Laughs A Lot Mermaid*

I am most at home where the wild things are.
—*Sister Ursula Divine Mermaid*

Sing, dance, create. If you have to choose one, do all three at once.
—*Sister Bridget Mermaid*

A good bean is hard to find. Everything else is easy.
—*Sister Ruby Rosarita Mermaid*

Go with the flow—and watch out for waterfalls.
—*Sister Sophia Mermaid*

You ask me to tell you about love? Showing is so much better.
—*Sister Magdelene Mermaid*

Laugh or weep. We swim in your tears.
—*Grand Mother Yemaya Mermaid*
All the wisdom of the ages can be distilled into one suggestion: Be.
—*Mother Star Stupendous Mermaid*

The rest is mystery.
—*Sister Faye Mermaid*

Gift

The Old Mermaids gift you with joy on this day. Take it in; it's yours.

Old Mermaid Suggestion

"Step lightly. Dance hard. Eat your vegetables."

—*Sister DeeDee Lightful Mermaid*

Recipe

Calling on Health and Prosperity

Get a tiny bowl, tiny, tiny—like a prep bowl. Put a little bit of honey in it—as much as you would put in a cup of tea. Now sprinkle a tiny amount of cinnamon powder on the honey. Mix them together. Imagine yourself protected and in good health. Whisper a chant if you like. Try this one, a variant of an old Croatian song:

A pinch of cinnamon
From my tin.

So sweet and sunny
Mixed with honey.

In my hot tea
May you protect me.
Bring true wealth
Which is good health.

    Then mix it in your tea, hot water, or spread it on toast, imagining all the while that you are healthy and prosperous.

Old Mermaid Tale

Bear Woman and Sister DeeDee Lightful Mermaid

After the Old Mermaids washed ashore on the New Desert, they had to quickly learn to survive. Although some were afraid, they didn't have much time for reflection or for many more tears. Their world had ended. All they had known was gone. They had each other—and the New Desert and the Old Neighbors.

With the help of the Old Neighbors, the Old Mermaids built their house, planted a garden, and established the Old Mermaids Sanctuary. It was a wonder to behold. Each Old Mermaid had her place in this new world.

Some of them stumbled now and again. After they all seemed to settle in, after they seemed to have accepted their fate, after nearly all of them adjusted to their new life, Sister DeeDee Lightful Mermaid realized she was not herself. She did not delight in anything.

This was such a new feeling for her that she didn't know what to do or what not to do. One day as she was walking in the desert beneath the seemingly unrelenting Sun, she heard a crow fly overhead. She heard the whoosh, whoosh, whoosh of the crow's wings in the dry air. She looked up and watched the bird fly toward Woman's Crying Summit. She decided to follow the bird.

She kept waiting for the crow to disappear from her view, but it didn't. Whenever she lagged behind, the crow would alight on something taller than either of them and wait for her. Eventually after an hour, a day, a week, a month, they were up the side of the mountain amongst pine trees. The crow perched on top of one and stayed there.

Sister DeeDee Lightful Mermaid stopped and looked around. Now what? Nothing happened. The Sun moved slowly across the sky. The crow groomed itself. Sister DeeDee Lightful Mermaid still did not feel like herself. She started to think about returning home. Then she heard a stirring in the leaves. She looked over and saw a Bear Woman standing not far from her. Or maybe it was a Bear. Or a Woman. She wasn't certain. Bears were new to her, although Sister Ursula Divine Mermaid had told her about a bear she had met on the mountains. Was this the same one?

"You have come to Bear Country," Bear Woman said. "Do you wish to die or know yourself better?"

"I want to feel better," Sister DeeDee Lightful Mermaid said.

"That was not one of the choices," Bear Woman said.

"I long for the Old Sea," Sister DeeDee Lightful Mermaid said.

Bear Woman nodded. "Of course. You miss the darkness.

Come. I will lend you mine. It is not watery, but it is what I have."

Sister DeeDee Lightful Mermaid followed Bear Woman to a cave in the mountainside. Bear Woman pointed to the darkness. "Is this what you need?"

"In the darkness, I shine," Sister DeeDee Lightful Mermaid said. "In the light, I am invisible."

"And this bothers you?" Bear Woman asked.

"I suppose it does," Sister DeeDee Lightful Mermaid said.

"I will keep the others away," Bear Woman said. "The creatures of the night, as it were. But other monsters may reside within."

Sister DeeDee Lightful Mermaid nodded. She understood. She stepped into the darkness. When her eyes adjusted, she still saw nothing. She felt around until her hands found a giant bed in the middle of this cave of darkness. Sister DeeDee Lightful Mermaid climbed into the bed.

She sat for an hour, a day, a month, a year. She breathed in the darkness and breathed out the darkness. She was relieved to be away from the harsh light of the Sun.

At some point, she heard a kind of buzzing in the room or a whirring of tiny wings. She held her fingers out to the darkness and something landed on one of her fingers. It was so light she could barely feel the claws clutching her finger.

"Let there be light," she whispered. And suddenly the thing on her finger was illuminated, as though a multicolored flame had been lit from within. A blue-green hummingbird was perched on her finger and now watched her intently. It was one of the most beautiful sights Sister DeeDee Lightful Mermaid had ever seen and she had seen much beauty in her life. Joy surged through her body.

Then she heard—from the bird?—"Let there be light." She looked down, and she was glowing from within, too. She smiled.

"I am myself again," she said.

The hummingbird flew away. Sister DeeDee Lightful Mermaid followed it out of the cave and into the sunshine. Bear

Woman and the crow were gone, but the day was young. She could get home before dinner. She hurried down the slope of the mountain.

    I won't say Sister DeeDee Lightful Mermaid never had any trouble again, because she did now and again, but gradually she began to feel at home in her body and in the New Desert. And when she didn't, she found darkness to wrap around her.

Poetry by Mario Milosevic

Black Coverings

The crow and the bear:
both wear darkness
for their overcoats.

They find solace in the night
when the light of the world
has retreated to the centers

of their beings, awaiting
the morning for full
flower and warming glory.

Action

Be full of yourself. You can do it.

And a Little Herstory

The name for Sister DeeDee Lightful Mermaid evolved from Atargatis, an ancient goddess of Syria. I wanted to have as many mermaid goddess names as possible for the Old Ems. The story goes that Atargatis came down from heaven in an egg and emerged from it as a mermaid. In one tale, she dives into a lake and becomes fish mother. She was also a vegetative goddess, sky goddess, and sea goddess.

The Greeks called Atargatis "Derceto." In Rome, they referred to Atargatis as "Dea Syria." Somehow when I read that all those years ago that made me think of "DeeDee Lightful."

I am also reminded of the Japanese Sun goddess Amaterasu when I think of Sister DeeDee Lightful Mermaid. Amaterasu hides herself in a cave and won't come out. The world falls into darkness. She is finally tricked into leaving the cave when the other gods hang a mirror right outside her cave. She sees her brilliant reflection and tries to get closer to it, naturally. They grab her hand, pull her out of the cave, and seal the cave for all time. Light is restored to the world.

Day Three
Day of the Hummingbird

December 22

The hummingbird is strictly a New World bird with different symbolic meanings depending upon the culture. To the Aztecs, the hummingbird was the Sun and war god Huitzilopochtli who avenged his mother's death. The Aztecs also believed hummingbirds were reincarnated warriors. To the Mayans, the hummingbird was the Sun in disguise (the black Sun, i.e. the eclipsed

Sun). The Hopi tell a story of the hummingbird shaming a god into making it rain again to assuage the suffering of the people.

In other cultures, the hummingbird is associated with love and healing. It is said their song or the whirring of their wings awakens the medicine in flowers. I love that idea. Every time a hummingbird is near, can you just imagine all the medicine awakening in the flowers and plants around us?

I feel a sense of joy and magic every time I see a hummingbird. The Old Mermaids felt the same way.

One early summer morning, Sister Lyra Musica Mermaid was out walking the wash with Sister Magdelene Mermaid. The sky was perfectly clear and so blue it almost hurt to look at it as it seemed to curve above the trees growing at the edge of the wash.

Both Old Ems heard the sound of hummingbird wings just as the tiny bird flew right over their heads. Not far behind, a red-tailed hawk came, looking huge and dangerous so close to the hummingbird, its hooked beak ready to tear out the smaller animal's innards. Sissy Maggie Mermaid called out in fear for the hummingbird.

Just then the hummingbird whirled around, hung in the air, and faced the hawk. The raptor stopped abruptly and hovered in the air, just feet from the hummingbird. It was only for a moment or two, but the Old Mermaids were in awe. The tiny colorful bird faced the huge hawk who could have killed it in an instant. Then, just like that, the red-tailed hawk flapped its wings and flew up and away. The hummingbird stayed its ground—as it were—in the air for another second or two, and then it flew away, too, in the opposite direction.

"See," Sissy Maggie said as she linked arms with Sister Lyra Musica Mermaid. "Sometimes we have to face that which wants to eat us alive."

In some traditions, the third day of Yule is a time to celebrate courage. From a human point of view, courage is demonstrated when we do something right even when we are terrified; true courage is when we do something right even when others taunt us and wish us ill. Courage is when we stand up for ourselves—just like the hummingbirds—and get what we need—and they do it all with beauty.

Dreams

Did birds enter your dreams by any chance? Or did the Sun or Moon visit your dreamland? Were you brave in your dreams? Try drawing an image from your dreams today. If you start to draw and don't remember enough details, close your eyes and step back into the dream and fill it out. Exercise that "daydream" muscle. Dreams are gifts from the Universe, the Ancestors, or your own wonderful self. Have fun with them.

Ground and Center

Send your roots deep into the Earth and find the Earth's center and your own. You've been doing this for three days now. How does it feel?

Look for Guides and Signs

Watch for birds today. Are you getting any messages from them or because of them? Maybe if a crow comes closer to you than usual, you are reminded of mystery in your life. Or if you see a robin, you think spring is closer than you imagined—maybe you are about to feel renewed yourself and experience your own spring. Push past your own fears and insecurities, and listen deeply. This is a way to let your true amazing wisdom come through.

Ceremony

Elemental Storytelling

In elemental magic, we honor air, fire, water, and earth as necessities for life. We can honor these elements through storytelling, too. Winter Solstice is the time of year for stories and storytelling. Being able to tell a story out loud is an ancient skill that many tried to cultivate. Stories help ground us, open up our imaginations, and connect us with our world.

Let's begin with air.

Think about air. If you have a feather, hold it in your hand as you contemplate air. Ask yourself when in your life was air particularly important to you. Did a lack of it or an overabundance of it (as in wind) affect you in some way? If you wish, take a few notes on your memory. Think about what you would say if you were talking about this with someone. Figure out how to tell it like a story with a beginning, middle, and end. How would you set the scene? Is there a climax to the incident: when everything went haywire or became beautiful? And how did it end? In storytelling, you don't want to tell every detail. You only want to share what is interesting and what moves the tale forward.

    The incident can be small or big. When I think of air, I sometimes remember having trouble breathing on the way home from a walk one day. I didn't have my inhaler, and I had to walk up a big hill. It was a beautiful spring day in the Columbia River Gorge, and I was missing my mother who had recently died. My chest kept tightening as I tried to walk up this hill. I couldn't catch my breath. I was alone, and I felt completely vulnerable. I didn't know how I was going to make it home—which was just over the hill.

I wondered if I was going to spend the rest of my life dealing with this issue. If I had a "rest of my life." I could die right here and now. I didn't know what to do.

Suddenly I noticed the plants on the side of the road, in the ditch: chicory, Queen Anne's Lace, and what we used to call honey when I was growing up: self-heal or prunella vulgaris. I stopped and stared at these plants. I felt as though they had called out to me. It wasn't in words. It was as if the Universe said, "You are not alone," and showed me these plants. I watched them. I told them how afraid I was. They told me all would be well. Mostly though, I just breathed with them, standing there on the sloping asphalt, the blue sky above me, a bunch of condos behind me.

Eventually, my chest opened up a bit, I said goodbye to the plants, and I made it up the hill to home. Ever since then, I know that I am never alone. I can step outside wherever I am, and I'll find a plant nearby, even if it's a dandelion coming up through the crack in the sidewalk. Life prevails, and life connects.

That's my story of air. What's yours?

Once you have your incident, your story, save it for tomorrow when we'll do more with it then.

Magic

Get up just before dawn. Dress warm. Bring a rattle with you. If you don't have one, put a few beans or pills in a jar and use that. Go outside and face the east. As the Sun begins to come up over the horizon, shake your rattle and sing, "Up, Sun, up! We admire you. We love you. We need you. Up, Sun, up!" Or create your own chant. When the Sun rises, cheer. Then hurry inside.

If it's too cold out or you don't feel comfortable cheering for the Sun publicly, you can do this indoors. Just find a window where you can see the Sun. Wherever you are, feel good that you helped the Sun rise on the morning after Solstice.

Gift

Stories are the gift to you from all the Old Mermaids but especially from Sister Lyra Musica Mermaid.

Old Mermaid Suggestion

"Fear has no sisters, but I have many."

—*Sister Lyra Musica Mermaid*

Recipe

Protective Magic Potatoes

This is a quick and easy recipe if you just want to do a little kitchen witchery or a little Old Mermaid magic with potatoes. Every recipe is just a spell in action, an outline of how to transform a group of ingredients into one whole dish. The idea is to cook with intention. Food is like all healing modalities: What heals one person might make another person groggy, or what heals one person might make another person sick to her stomach. Ask the plant. For instance, perhaps rosemary is known to be a protector herb in some places in the world, but in your yard, it feels like it's a love herb. Everyone is different. Every plant is different for every person.

For this recipe, you will need:

- 2 potatoes (for two servings)
- salt
- butter or oil
- Milk, coconut milk, or water
- Any other herbs or spices you want to use

Hold the potatoes in your hands. Close your eyes. Imagine the potatoes nourishing you. Imagine the spirit of the potato plant protecting you. Imagine you are in good health after eating the potato. Ask the spirit of the potato plant to protect you.

At this point, make mashed potatoes however you make mashed potatoes. While you are doing it, stay relaxed, keep imagining yourself protected, healthy, and grounded. Then eat them as your main dish in a meal or make them a side dish for a meal.

If you don't have your own way to make mashed potatoes, try this: After you've briefly held the potatoes and asked for protection, wash them, peel them, cut them into cubes, and then put them in a pot of water and bring it to a boil. When a fork goes through them easily, drain the water, and put the potatoes in a bowl. Mash them up. Salt to taste. Put in a little milk, coconut milk, or water if it's too dry. Add some butter or a little olive oil to give it more taste. Just keep tasting it until you like it. Add chives, scallions, garlic, or whatever else you like.

Then sit down and eat it, knowing the whole time that you are protected.

Poetry by Mario Milosevic

Holding Your Ground

No one remembers
their audacious first breath,

that initial impulse
for survival. Tasting

this foreign atmosphere,
thinnest of soup

after the amniotic
bounty of the womb.

Such courage to
meet the world

with untested wings,
air inflating your lungs,

light animating your eyes,
and your voice: cries

darting into the ears of
everyone everywhere.

Action

Sing! Play music! Focus on a goal.

Day Four
Day of the Bean

December 23

In the Sonoran Desert around the Old Mermaids Sanctuary, every other tree or bush seems to be a legume. Bean pods hang from branches everywhere at this time of year, like Nature's own holiday decorations. The Old Ems and their neighbors delighted in beans. Whenever Sister Ruby Rosarita Mermaid made bean soup, she would sing, "Beans, beans, we're mermaid queens," as she stirred the pot.

When Sister Ruby Rosarita Mermaid reminds us that we are queens, she is singing about a queen who is ruler of herself, not someone who is ruling others. She knows her realms, and she celebrates this knowledge.

So on this Day of the Bean, celebrate your realms. And fill yourself up with some delicious nourishing food.

Dreams

Have you dreamed about food or plants lately? Have you ever dreamed of food or plants? If not, sit quietly in bed before you get up, or take some time during the day when you can be alone and quiet. Set your intention to daydream about a plant or about food and see where that takes you. Let the daydream spool out without trying to control it. When you are finished, write out what you experienced. You might find a message in your daydream.

Ground and Center

As you ground and center this morning and your roots go down into the Earth, be aware of plant roots all around you. As you are rooted, they are rooted, and as they are rooted, so are you. We are all rooted on this Earth together.

Look for Guides and Signs

Be aware. Nature is talking with you. It doesn't mean you'll find all the answers in this conversation, but it will be a nice talk.

Ceremony

Whatever you cook today, cook with purpose and attention. Thank the food. I once dreamed of this old Rumanian woman who was cooking and teaching me while she cooked. She made motions with her hands and murmured prayers. She told me, "You should always talk to the spirits in everything." And so, today (if not every day), thank the stove for the heat, thank all the ingredients for the meal you make, and thank all the hands that were involved in getting this meal to your table.

Magic

Elemental Storytelling

You have your story about air from yesterday. Say it out loud. Yes, tell your story out loud. Tell it to yourself. If you're not used to speaking out loud much, this will be strange for you. Do it anyway. Once you say it out loud, determine which parts of the tale you can drop and what more you need to bring in. Then, if you like, tell the story to someone else. Storytelling *is* magic. Use your words as an enchantment to create a better world.

Gift

Along with all the other Old Ems, Sister Ruby Rosarita Mermaid gifts you with enough to eat. May all you eat heal and nourish you.

Old Mermaid Suggestion

"A good bean is hard to find. Everything else is easy."

—*Sister Ruby Rosarita Mermaid*

Recipe for Bean Soup

It seems bean soup turns up in a lot of my works, including the recipe by Crane in *Coyote Cowgirl*. This recipe is very similar to the one in *Coyote Cowgirl*. This one was suggested by an Old Mermaids Sanctuary visitor from Mexico who would never tell the Old Ems her name. She called herself the Visitor, so Sister Ruby Rosarita Mermaid nicknamed her, "Vee," and the Visitor was OK with that. Vee encouraged Sister Ruby to play with the recipe once she had given it to her. "Listen to the beans," Vee said. "They can be quite the *parlanchin*—quite the chatterbox."

Ingredients:

- 3 cups dried pinto beans (rinse and soak overnight).
- 3 tablespoons oil (olive or whatever you like when sautéing)
- 10-20 good garlic cloves, minced or pressed
- 3 medium yellow onions, coarsely chopped
- 3 cups peeled and chopped fresh tomatoes or about 28 ounces of peeled chopped tomatoes in a jar (this can be optional)
- ½ teaspoon coriander or several sprigs of fresh chopped cilantro

Rinse and drain the beans after you've soaked them; let them sit for 30 minutes. Don't forget to talk to the food all during the soup-making process. Soup is especially magical and healing.

Heat the oil in a large pot. When a drop of water sizzles on the oil, add the pinto beans. Sauté them for 4-5 minutes, making sure you're stirring most of the time so they don't stick. Add more oil if they stick too much. Add 8-10 cups of water or about double the level of the beans. Add more water or let some water boil off depending upon what consistency of soup you want. Simmer for four hours. After four hours add onions and garlic. Cook another hour, and then add tomatoes and coriander. Cook another hour. If you want to be nightshade-free, omit the tomatoes, but keep cooking the beans.

After about six hours, see if the beans are done. Add seasoning if needed. If you don't use tomatoes, it tends to need some salt.

Serve as a stand alone soup with grated Monterey Jack cheese or a cheese substitute (or none at all—it's very rich and creamy). If you eat bread, it's great with bread.

Old Mermaid Tale

Visitor's Bean Soup

The Visitor first came to the Old Mermaids Sanctuary soon after Winter Solstice. I can't be certain, but it may have even been the first winter the Old Ems spent out of the Old Sea and in the New Desert. They were not accustomed to the changes in the weather: Now they felt the cold much more deeply than they ever did in the Old Sea. Some evenings, they could barely stop shivering.

On one of those evenings, Vee—as Sister Ruby Rosarita Mermaid called The Visitor—suggested they make The Bean Soup from a bag of beans the Old Neighbors had brought over the day before. That's all she called it: The Bean Soup. Or *sopa de fríjol*. In her village, she told them as she picked out stones from the beans, "this sopa could bring fighting lovers back together and warm any chill in any heart."

Vee instructed Sister Bea Wilder Mermaid to rinse the beans and put them in a big pot. Then Sister Sophia Mermaid poured water over the beans and turned on the stove.

"In some countries," Vee said, "only the magic people can cook beans. But here—" She shrugged. "—here we are all magic."

And so the beans and water bubbled for hours and hours while the Old Mermaids sat around telling stories to each other.

Eventually Vee called for *ajo*—garlic—and onions. "For protection," she said. "One can rarely have enough protection."

"From what?" Sister Magdelene Mermaid asked.

"From whatever will ail us or flail us," Vee said.

Later, she cut up tomatoes and put them in the bean soup. "These are for love," she said. "We can't get enough love either."

"I agree!" Sister Magdelene Mermaid said.

The aromas from the bean soup filled the house. Sister Sheila Na Giggles Mermaid opened a door, and a breeze ran through the house and carried the delicious smells out to all the neighbors. Soon enough—just about the time the beans were done—Old Neighbors from all around came streaming into the house.

"What is that delicious smell?" they asked. "We assumed it had to be an invitation to dinner."

"Of course!" Sister Ruby Rosarita Mermaid said.

As often happened in the Old Mermaids Sanctuary, a meal became a feast. The sopa de fríjol never ran out. No one was quarreling, so they didn't know if that part of the magic of the soup worked or not. They did all agree that they loved it. And the Old Mermaids were no longer cold.

Poetry by Mario Milosevic

Light Beans

Behold the beauty
of the pod's journey

from branch to ground.
How the beans nestle

in the groove, awaiting
liberation. Later the

critters coming round
to taste the bounty,

pod and bean crunching
audibly against their teeth

like branches snapping.
Nothing broken here.

The beams of strength
and nutrition hold their

regal place in the world
like a queen's crown.

Action

Eat something wonderful and healing today.

And a Little Herstory

Sister Ruby Rosarita Mermaid was named after Our Lady of the Roses who is the Virgin Mary who is also Stella Maris: Our Lady, Star of the Sea. Although Stella Maris is not a mermaid, she is connected with the Old Sea. Because of her name, Sister Ruby Rosarita Mermaid is also linked to the goddess of the Americas, the Virgin of Guadalupe, who is the pre-Hispanic goddess Tonantzin and/or Cihuacóatl, the protector of women.

Day Five
Day of the Deer

December 24

Most of us have some experience with deer, either in stories or in real life. They are incredibly adaptable and thrive almost everywhere on Earth except Australia. Nearly every culture has some folklore centered on deer, perhaps because deer were such a reliable food source. Clarissa Pinkola Estés says that the sacrifice of a deer—especially a doe—was the work of the "ancient Wild Woman bloodline." It was a rite of revivification: The sacrifice of the deer renewed life. It was a way of becoming the deer: the Deer Woman. This is heady stuff.

Nowadays, I don't feel as though we need to sacrifice a deer to delve into the Deer Woman mysteries. We can ask the spirit and soul of the deer what we need to sacrifice—to make sacred—to hear and understand her teachings.

Dreams

Has the antlered one come to you yet? Have you ever dreamed of deer? Do you remember the dream? What did it mean to you then? What would it mean to you now?

If you have dreamed of deer lately, explore the dream to find its meaning. If you haven't, daydream a deer visit. Go somewhere quiet and still, close your eyes, and imagine you are dreaming of a deer. Does the deer have a message for you?

If you don't have time for this today, don't worry about it. The deer will let you know if she needs to contact you.

Ground and Center

Let your roots go deep and bring up that healing energy today. If this is an especially busy day, it's particularly a good idea to ground and center. If it's a sad day because of whatever reasons, it's a particularly good idea to ground and center, too.

Look for Guides and Signs

Watch for deer and deer energy today. It's out there even if you don't see any signs in Nature. Maybe you want to temporarily disappear or be very, very still. Maybe you have the urge to shapeshift into Deer Woman. What would that mean for you?

Ceremony

Elemental Storytelling

You may wonder why I put storytelling under Ceremony. I could put it under Magic or Recipe, too. It would fit under all three. I think of storytelling as ritual and ceremony. You make a quiet space for yourself. You ask for help from the Creative Forces, and then you remember. You put the pieces together to come up with a story. That feels like a ritual to me, or a ceremony. And it's also a magical recipe.

So to continue our elemental stories: Find that quiet place and space, ask the Universe or your higher self or the Creative

Forces to be with you as you dip into your memories. Think of an incident in your life that involves fire. Jot down the details. Figure out which parts of it will make a good story. A beginning, middle, end. Say it out loud to yourself. Then play with it to find the right rhythm.

We had an Old Mermaids School of Telling Tales for a while when I lived in Washington. We did these same exercises. Each night we would think about air or water or fire or earth, and then we would tell a story from our lives.

I still remember one story my friend Evine, who was in her eighties then, told us about a fire event when she was a child. She and her parents and siblings had recently moved out into the country in Oregon. The house was not finished. In fact, not all of the walls of the house were up yet, so it didn't afford them much protection.

Her father had to go away. That night while her father was gone, wolves came to their home site and surrounded them. Her mother hid her siblings in boxes in the house, and then she and

Evine stayed outside building the fire higher and higher to keep the wolves at bay. Evine said she could still see the fire in the wolves' eyes. The fire kept the wolves away, and the family survived the night.

This method of storytelling is also a wonderful way to get people to talk about themselves. You can go around the room and have each person tell a tale about fire—or one of the other elements—and it usually turns out that they are sharing an important part of themselves with the group.

Magic

Your magic today is your fire story. And if you celebrate Christmas, carry out your Christmas Eve tasks with a sense of wonder: make it all magic.

Gift

Your gift today is laughter.

Old Mermaid Suggestion

"She who laughs a lot laughs a lot."

—Sister Laughs a Lot Mermaid

Old Mermaid Tale

The Girl Who Didn't Speak and the Tea Party

One day, a young mother and her seven-year-old daughter stumbled into the Old Mermaids Sanctuary. Their eyes were glassy, their clothes torn and tattered, their shoes falling apart.

The Old Mermaids brought them food and drink, treated their cuts and scrapes, and took them indoors when they were ready.

The mother's name was Gimena, and the girl was called Ichika. After they had bathed and rested, they sat outside by the pool and garden, and Gimena told the Old Ems that they had come from a place of war. Her husband had been captured by gangs. As her husband was dragged away, he shouted, "I will meet you where the sea ends and the magic begins." Gimena feared they would come back for her and her daughter, so she left.

"I have been looking for a place where the sea ends and magic begins for many days and weeks now," Gimena said. With tears in her eyes, she asked, "Do you think this is the place? Have you seen my husband? His name is Ain. He has one blue eye and one brown eye. The grandmothers in our village used to say he was blessed and could see into two worlds at once. But the grandmothers are no more, and my husband is—" She glanced over at Ichika who sat near the pool staring into the bottom of it. She had not said a word since the Old Mermaids met her. "My husband is missing from our lives."

Grand Mother Yemaya Mermaid said, "We are so sorry for your troubles. This is a place where the Old Sea ended, and we have our share of magic. So perhaps this is the place. You are welcome to stay here as long as you like."

And so Gimena and her daughter Ichika came to live at the Old Mermaids Sanctuary for a time. Gimena helped the Old Mermaids out at the Tea Shell, where she served special teas, sopas, and desserts to all the Old Neighbors. At first Ichika stayed close to her mother, but after a while she also spent time with the Old Mermaids. She never said a word. She just stayed near, helping them out in the kitchen or garden or when they went to visit their neighbors. She went with them to birthday celebrations. She helped Sissy Maggie sew new clothes for them. At night sometimes, she sat with Mother Star Stupendous Mermaid and Grand Mother Yemaya Mermaid as they gazed up at the sky and pointed out stars to one another.

Still she said nothing.

One evening Ichika and Sister Laughs a Lot Mermaid were walking back from a community dinner at Annie Who Loves Birds' house. The other Old Mermaids and Gimena were either ahead of them or behind them. After a while Ichika and Sister Laughs a Lot Mermaid sat on the bench near the fork in the wash. It had been a long and tiring day.

La Luna rose in the sky, and it seemed suddenly and all at once and over an eon that silver light bathed the desert. Just then Ichika and Sister Laughs a lot Mermaid heard something peculiar. It sounded like the clinking of glass against glass or fork against plate.

What on Earth?

Ichika and Sister Laughs a Lot Mermaid got up and began walking quietly to the wash. The sound grew louder, and now they could hear voices. They went down into the wash and began walking. The dry river curved a bit. And then they saw it, in a stream of Moonlight, right there where they came to the fork in the wash: Sitting around a long wooden table with tea cups and platters of cookies and cupcakes and little sandwiches was a deer (or a deer woman), a jack rabbit or two, several bunny rabbits, a javelina, a pack rat, and a bobcat. They were all eating and drinking and talking, just like humans. In fact, they looked like people and animals all at the same time.

Sister Laughs a Lot Mermaid blinked and looked down at Ichika. Her eyes were wide. Sister Laughs a Lot Mermaid had seen many wondrous things in her life, but she had never seen a tea party with wild animals.

And these animals were dressed in the most ornate and beautiful clothes either of them had ever seen on any creature. The deer or woman wore a gold coat with all sorts of jewels catching the light and glittering each time she moved. Pack Rat or pack rat woman had on a purple top hat that matched her deep purple waistcoat. The jackrabbits and bunny rabbits only wore vests, but each vest was unique in its coloring and the design on the back. The javelina sported what looked like a pink velvet dress.

"This is the Deer Mother," Sister Laughs a Lot Mermaid whispered to Ichika. "I have heard stories of her."

The deer looked over at the Old Mermaid and the girl just then. "Ah, dear ones," she said. "Come. Join us."

Ichika looked up at Sister Laughs a Lot Mermaid who nodded. The two walked over to the table in the sand. Deer Mother pointed to the two empty chairs next to one another.

"We have been waiting for you," Deer Mother said. Sister Laughs a Lot Mermaid and Ichika sat on the wooden chairs with animals carved into every inch of them.

"We have?" Bobcat Man asked.

"We have," Jackrabbit said.

"Eat and drink," Javelina grumbled.

Sister Laughs a Lot Mermaid and Ichika both put goodies and sandwiches on their plates. They had never heard that one should not eat and drink in Fairyland or one might never be able to leave. Of course, some might argue that the Old Mermaids Sanctuary was part of Fairyland, hook, line, and sinker, as it were.

"I have never seen this before," Sister Laughs a Lot Mermaid said, "a table in the wash."

Deer Mother nodded. "I got tired of the wild life," she said. "So here we are."

The others around the table laughed. Sister Laughs a Lot Mermaid smiled and looked at Ichika who was biting into a chocolate cupcake.

"Beware, child," Deer Mother said. "Chocolate is powerful magic."

"Magic doesn't exist," Ichika said, her mouth filled with cupcake.

Ah, she had finally spoken.

Everyone around the table laughed again.

"Uh-oh," Bunny Rabbit said. "I guess that means I don't exist." She snapped her fingers, and she disappeared. Ichika's eyes widened. Deer Mother snapped her fingers and Bunny Rabbit reappeared.

"Rude," Deer Mother said. "One mustn't disappear without notice."

And so they ate and told stories. Jackrabbit spoke about the many times he and his people danced in this same wash under the full Moon. Pack Rat remembered when the rancher destroyed her home. "It had been in my family for 40,000 years." Bobcat Man talked about the time his mother was killed by a hunter when he was just a cub. He barely survived. The others cried quietly when he described his life.

Then Deer Mother said, "We raise a cup to Bobcat Man's mother." They each held up their tea cup—including Ichika. "May Bobcat Man's mother continue to hunt in wide open places. And may Pack Rat's new home last for 40,000 years."

"Here, here," Javelina said.

The stories continued until it seemed everyone got their fill of treats, tea, sandwiches, and the cultivated life.

Then Deer Mother said, "It is time to return to the wild life, my friends."

She stood and pulled a small moonlight-colored bag from inside her glittery coat. Then she reached around the table and took cookies, small cupcakes, and colored ball candy and dropped them into the bag. Sister Laughs a Lot Mermaid and Ichika got up from the table and walked around to the Deer Mother.

"Thank you, all," Sister Laughs a Lot Mermaid said. "This was a lovely tea party."

The others nodded and said things like, "Of course," "any time," "our pleasure."

Deer Mother handed Ichika the bag filled with treats.

"Thank you, Deer Mother," Ichika said.

Deer Mother gently put her hand under Ichika's chin.

"You are welcome, dear one."

And then a cloud went over the Moon. Or someone snapped their fingers. The tea party was gone. In the next moment, Sister Laughs a Lot Mermaid and Ichika opened their eyes, and they were sitting on the bench near the fork in the dry river in the dark. The two looked at each other.

"It was all a dream?" Ichika asked.

Sister Laughs a Lot Mermaid shrugged. "A wonderful dream that we both had. We better get home before your mother worries."

Sister Laughs a Lot Mermaid stood and reached for Ichika's hand. The girl held up the bag Deer Mother had given her. It was still full of treats.

"It was not a dream," Ichika said. She grabbed Sister Laughs a Lot Mermaid's hand with her other hand, and they hurried home, running when they could see well enough, walking quickly when they couldn't, laughing and remembering the tea party.

When they got to the Old Mermaids Sanctuary and the house, Ichika dropped Sister Laughs a Lot Mermaid's hand and ran through the door into the lighted house.

"Momma!" Ichika cried. "I have brought you magic."

Sister Laughs a Lot Mermaid followed the child into the house. All the sister mermaids were crowded around Gimena. They moved out of the way to make room for the running child, and Sister Laughs a Lot Mermaid could see a man sitting next to Gimena.

"Poppa!" Ichika cried as she jumped into her father's lap, still holding tightly to the bag. Her father wrapped his arms around his daughter and held her tightly.

"We brought treats from the Deer Mother's tea party," Ichika said. She held the bag out to Grand Mother Yemaya Mermaid.

"Wonderful," Grand Mother said.

"Let me tell you about the tea party," Ichika said. "You wouldn't believe it. Except for right now seeing Poppa, it was the most wonderful thing I've ever seen."

Ichika told her parents and the Old Ems about their night while Sister Ruby Rosarita Mermaid and Sister Sheila Na Giggles Mermaid brought them tea. They all ate treats from the moonlight bag which stayed full until Ichika finished her story and they had all had their fill.

Poetry by Mario Milosevic

A Gift of Fire

I see the slow motion smoke
of antlers rising
from the flaming camouflage
of your patterned skull.
You bend your head,
silent bow,
drop the branched horns
to the ground,
then retreat to the woods,
blazing with autumn color.
You are the gift-giver:
sparking gratitude,
aloof and melting
into anonymity's safety.

Action

Laugh and have fun.

And a Little Herstory

Sister Laughs a Lot Mermaid is a kind of incarnation of Baubo. Remember her from the Demeter myth? Demeter was in mourning over the loss of her daughter, and no plants would grow, no flowers bloomed.

Then one day, a cleaning woman (who was really the goddess Baubo) lifted her skirts and revealed what was underneath. Demeter smiled and then began to laugh. As she laughed, the Earth came alive again.

In my book *The Salmon Mysteries: A Guidebook to a Reimagining of the Eleusinian Mysteries,* Baubo is portrayed by Coyote, the trickster. Sister Laughs a Lot Mermaid is a bit of a trickster herself. I can see her walking around lifting her skirts now and again.

Day Six

Day of the Sun

December 25

Merry Christmas! May it be a beautiful and joyous day for you. For millions of Christians around the world, this is the day to celebrate the birth of the son. For many people in our culture, this is an extremely busy day. Enjoy it, if you can. Be aware of the magic of the day. If you are away from your loved ones, be kind to yourself. Do something comforting and fun if you can.

Dreams

The light continues to grow. Has any light come into your dreams? How can you become "enlightened" today? If you have time today, daydream about light.

Ground and Center

Today when you do the Healing Roots Meditation, imagine that healing light from the Sun is flowing into the top of your head. As the energy from the center of the Earth comes up through your roots, so the healing energy of the Sun also pours into your body and fills every cell with good health. The two energies flow peacefully and cooperatively through your body, creating a kind of loop that fills every part of your body. When you feel "full," let the energies go, releasing the Sun energy first. It flows peacefully up and away. Then release the Earth energy.

Look for Guides and Signs

Any new insights yet? Was there something you believed for a long time that you now realize wasn't true or wasn't exactly the way you thought it was? This is a sign that you are preparing to move forward into the new year.

Ceremony

This is a busy day in many households, so take some time for yourself, even if it's only for five minutes. Try to get out into the Sun, light a candle, or do something which shines a light into the darkness. Express your gratitude for the light of the candle, the Sun, or electricity in any way you choose.

Magic

Elemental Storytime

Today would be a great time to tell your fire story to someone. If you're with other people in your household, it can be part of your conversation. "Hey, everyone, let's do elemental stories. Let's tell each other something that's happened to us that involves one of the elements, like fire. Does anyone have a memory of fire?" You can tell your story first as a way of encouraging others. If you are alone, say it out loud, to your cat or dog or to the Cosmos. Go outside and tell it. Nature loves a good story.

Gift

Wisdom. Remember what Sister Sophia Mermaid says, "Use your wisdom wisely."

Old Mermaid Suggestion

"Go with the flow—and watch out for waterfalls."

—*Sister Sophia Mermaid*

Recipe

Sister Sophia Mermaid sometimes tells people, "The best recipe for success is to let go of preconceived ideas about everything. Then the path to the truth will show itself to you. It's not always pleasant, but it's better to make choices and decisions based on reality." I should point out that the Old Mermaids' definition of success has nothing to do with money. It is about prosperity of the soul. For them, this means having good relations with the land and all the critters (human and otherwise)—and with the Cosmos in general.

Old Mermaid Tale

Solving Problems the Old Mermaids Way

All the Old Neighbors celebrated the return of the light at this time of year. Some of them decorated cacti or mesquite trees with colored ornaments they made, usually from paper and ribbon. After a few days, they would take the ornaments down—at least the ones the pack rats hadn't gotten—and put them away for next year or burn them in their fires on chilly mornings.

Sister Sophia Mermaid loved this time of the year because she had an excuse to make cookies in the Tea Shell all day long. She would talk to the dough as she made the cookies and add honey or sugar and spices and whisper or sing to them, too. "Keep everyone safe!" "May all be healthy!" "Bring joy to the world." And then she would name them: Safety Cookies. Healthy Cookies. Joyful Cookies. Everyone especially loved the cookies the Old Ems often served with Owl Identity Crisis Tea or Bunny Rabbits Love You Tea: Comfy Cookies.

Sometimes Sister Sophia Mermaid got a little cranky, no matter what time of year it was. She knew a lot, and she thought everyone else knew a lot, and sometimes people's questions seemed unwise.

One morning around the time of the Solstice, Sister Sophia Mermaid made cookies with chocolate chips some faery woman from the south had left the month before when she wandered through looking for her tribe. Sister Sophia Mermaid was able to show the faery woman—who never gave her name—where the veil between worlds had ripped—like a kind of esoteric hernia—and Faery Woman was able to follow her people into the rift. In gratitude, Faery Woman left little pieces of chocolate that were out of this world.

Sister Sophia Mermaid made cookies with this chocolate. She ate one as she piled the rest of them on a Tea Shell plate. They were pretty good chocolate chip cookies, but then, how could they not be: Sister Sophia Mermaid had made them, and they were full of faery chocolate.

Before she could come up with a name for them, Rancher Josephson strode into the Tea Shell. Sister Sophia Mermaid rolled her eyes. She was not in the mood for Rancher Josephson today. He always wanted to argue with her about something, and he never knew anything at all—even though he believed himself to be the smartest person in the world.

Rancher Josephson walked over to the counter where Sister Sophia Mermaid stood. He looked down at the plate full of cookies and asked, "Will eating one of these solve all my problems?"

Sister Sophia Mermaid wanted to say, "Of course not." Instead she answered, "Yes," without even a hint of sarcasm or irony in her voice.

Rancher Josephson put a cookie in his mouth all at once and began to chew. He nodded, said thank you with a full mouth, and left the Tea Shell without another word

"Well, that certainly solved all my problems," Sister Sophia Mermaid said. On the sign for the cookies, she wrote "Solve All Your Problems Cookies." Then she ate another cookie, just in case Rancher Josephson decided to come back.

Poetry by Mario Milosevic

Eclipse Blossom

The moon slowly
consumes the sun
leaving a black coin
at its center
and sprouting a crown
of shimmering petals
around its rim.
We remove
our cardboard glasses.
With unprotected eyes
we admire the bloom
of a star's atmosphere

electrifying the sky.
Twilight descends,
peaking for a brief time
before the moon moves on
heralding the return
of the light.

Action

Spread some true wisdom today.

And a Little Herstory

The story behind Sister Sophia Mermaid is pretty obvious: She is the embodiment of *sophia*, i.e. wisdom. Sophia has all kinds of stories attached to her. Some say she was the mother of God and others say she was the mother of Christ. I've heard her called the female Christ and the soul of the world. I used the name because it translates to wisdom, and Sister Sophia Mermaid is very wise—often cranky as many truly wise people are, impatient that they are surrounded by so many foolish people.

Day Seven

Day of the Bear

December 26

In some cultures even today, people believe humans are descended from bears, at least spiritually. In Siberia, the people felt so close to the bear that they would call him "Grandfather" as they hunted him. They pleaded with him not to hurt them; they had to kill him for their families.

Spiritually Bear is often thought of as the great healer. She goes to sleep every winter to regenerate—and to dream the world anew. Today is a good time for quiet and introspection. Be like the Bear, in whatever way that is for you.

Dreams

Welcome the wild things into your dreams. Did you dream of bear? I used to dream about bear frequently, several times a week. The dreams stopped, for the most part, after I promised Bear to write the novel *Her Frozen Wild*, about the shapechanging People.

In my dreams, Bear was often chasing me or my husband. In one dream, I looked down at my hands and saw I had grizzly bear claws. It was so great! In another dream, a bear was pillaging the whole neighborhood. When it broke into the house where I was, I faced him and offered myself up to save everyone.

He accepted. That was the end of the marauding bear nightmares.

Is there something in your dreams that you need to face? If you are having troubling dreams, try facing the problem in a daydream to see what can happen.

Ground and Center

Use the Healing Roots Meditation today, or if you like, try this new meditation. I call this the Merging Mountain Meditation. Jon Kabat-Zinn does a lovely Mountain Meditation. This is my version with some changes to his.

    Ground and center, close your eyes, and think of your favorite mountain or choose the first mountain that comes to mind. Watch it in your imagination. Breathe as you gaze upon it. Then ask if you can merge with it. If the answer is no, move on to another mountain and try again. Once you get a yes answer, breathe with the mountain and imagine you have merged with it so that you are now the mountain. Ahhh! Look all around. Enjoy the perspective. Feel what it's like to be something so old and solid. Imagine that it is spring on the mountain—on you; see and feel the changes. Imagine it is summer on the mountain—on you; note how the changes don't really make a difference to you as the mountain. They don't affect you. Imagine it is fall and then winter and then spring again. The Wheel of the Year has turned and many things change on and around you, but you are still you. The essence of you as the mountain has remained intact. When you are ready, merge back into the body of you meditating. Thank the mountain and then continue your day with the perspective of a mountain.

Look for Guides and Signs

Have any wild things crossed your path today? If so, if they were part of a dream you had, what would it mean? If not, daydream with a wild creature, perhaps even a bear.

Ceremony

Elemental Storytelling

Let's continue our Elemental Storytelling journey with water.

Find a quiet place. Ask your guides and helpers to remind you of a time when water meant something in your life, one memory that would make an interesting story. Once you have it, tell it to yourself. Write it down if you like. When you are ready, tell it to someone else. If you are alone, tell it to the cat, yourself, or someone on the phone. You don't need to recite every detail of the event, just choose details that set the scene and the mood.

I grew up in Michigan, so I have many memories of water.

One summer when I was a teen, my family stayed at my uncle's cabin up north, just as we had many times before. One day I sat on an air mattress in the lake for hours talking to a boy. Waves from boats racing by rocked us almost continuously. When I finally went back to the cabin, I felt like I was still on the water going up and down. It was disconcerting and nauseating. I was terrified it would never go away. I walked around the neighborhood for hours, until I started to feel normal. The whole thing scared me so much that I don't think I ever talked to that boy again.

For seven years, Mario and I lived in a neighborhood on the shores of the Columbia River. Nearly every year, the river behind us and the lake out front of our house flooded. Another year, the pipes froze and then burst. Water flooded the crawl space under the house where Mario went with a plumber who told him—once they were deep under the house—"I haven't done anything like this since my heart surgery."

In any case, I am certain you have many water stories, too, and you only need one.

Magic

Under Recipe today is a poem by Mario called "Cherry Crisp." It is actually a recipe for a cherry crisp. Cherries are reputedly great additions to successful love spells.

If you want to create a little love magic, think about love as you're making the crisp. Draw a heart with your finger in the bottom of the pan before you put the mixed ingredients into it. Every time you eat a piece of the crisp, think of love.

If you're more interested in protection than love, use blueberries instead of cherries. Instead of a heart, write with your finger in the bottom of the pan "protection." Every time you eat a piece of the blueberry crisp, think about how safe and protected you are.

Gift

Sister Ursula Divine Mermaid and all the Old Mermaids gift you with the knowledge of wild things. Use it well.

Old Mermaid Suggestion

"I am most at home where the wild things are."

—*Sister Ursula Divine Mermaid*

Recipe:

Cherry Crisp

Best to cut the cherries in
half to liberate the juices.

Spread them out in the pie pan.
Add a sprinkle of cinnamon.

Stir in a bit of maple syrup.
Set that aside for the moment.

You might want to admire
all those red half spheres

crowded in on one another

like some field of red tulips.

Now take a few generous
spoonfuls of coconut oil.

Melt them in the microwave
or the stove top until

the oil is clear and liquid.
Add the oil to a big scoop

full of quick cooking oats.
Stir that around until the

oats are coated with the oil
then spread the mixture

as though it were an overcast
sky onto that field of red

tulips you planted earlier.
Slide the whole creation

into a three hundred and
fifty degree oven to sun

bake the oats and the
cherries for about an hour.

Eat it warm or cool and
consider serving it with

a scoop or two of ice cream
because, well, ice cream!

—Mario Milosevic

Old Mermaid Tale

Cherry Crisp and Sister Ursula Divine Mermaid

At least once a year Sister Ursula Divine Mermaid would ask Sister Ruby Rosarita Mermaid to make a cherry crisp for her. Sister Ruby Rosarita Mermaid knew the crisp wasn't actually for Sister Ursula Divine Mermaid to eat herself, so she told her sister mermaid, "Only if you help me."

They almost always used cherries Annie Who Loves Birds had traded for art with someone who claimed to be an orchardist from way over yonder and beyond. The sister mermaids cherished the cherries and lovingly crafted a crisp from the cherries and oats and a little bit of sweetener.

Once Sister Ursula Divine Mermaid had the crisp in hand, she travelled up the mountains by herself. When she reached the cave of Bear Woman, she called out to her, but Bear Woman almost never answered. So Sister Ursula Divine Mermaid left the crisp at the entrance and then travelled back down the mountain to the Old Mermaids Sanctuary.

Bear had helped Sister Ursula Divine Mermaid find her true name when the Old Mermaids first came to the New Desert. Every year, Sister Ursula Divine Mermaid thanked the bear with a cherry crisp because she knew it was Bear Woman's favorite. And because it is always a good idea to honor the Ancestors.

Poetry by Mario Milosevic

Kinship

Sisters under the skin,
bear and mountain
understand each other.
They relish long sleeps,
instinctively take up space
with grace and power,
and know the value
of a striking profile.
Their wild hearts,
filled with strength,
are constant beacons
of authentic wisdom.

Action

Talk to a tree or a bear today—or merge with a mountain.

And a Little Herstory

Sister Ursula Divine Mermaid was named after Bear. The name Ursula is from the Latin word *ursa*, which means bear. The word divine means godlike and is related to the word deva. This is a reminder that all the Old Mermaids are goddesses.

Day Eight

Day of the Song

December 27

Late in December is a good time for song in the Sonoran desert, especially bird songs as the resident and wintering birds seem to find joy in the relatively mild weather. But any time is appropriate for song. We can find our voice especially during this Day of Song. Sing out your favorite tunes, even if it's just in the shower. If that's not comfortable, sing the vowels, one at a time. AEIOU. See how that feels. You deserve to be heard.

Dreams

How have your dreams been going? Are you suddenly dream-dry? Don't worry. This often happens when one takes a dreaming class or concentrates on dreaming. A little dry spell comes along before the flood begins. Or if you just aren't a dreamer and you haven't put a notebook by the side of the bed, try that now. As soon as you awaken in the morning, write down what you remember. If you don't remember anything, keep trying. Also stay off the computer and your phone for at least an hour before bed. If you can, try to awaken without an alarm clock. That alone will help you dream better.

Ground and Center

How is the grounding and centering going? Have you tried the Merging Mountain Meditation, too? If you're having difficulties doing the Healing Roots Meditation exercise, try having the root come out of your tailbone and see if that makes a difference.

Look for Guides and Signs

Today, listen for songs. You'll find them everywhere. I was at a workshop years ago. Everyone was asleep except me, since I always have trouble falling asleep when I'm away from home. I sat quietly. I heard what sounded like music—like drumming, only different somehow. In fact, it sounded like music somewhere in the house. I got out of my chair to explore. I had to find out where this faery music was coming from. I followed the sound . . . to the kitchen sink where the water was dripping into a pan. I was delighted. It was another lesson in how the ordinary is so extraordinary. I was able to go to sleep after that.

Ceremony

Elemental Storytelling

Once again find a quiet spot. Call in your guides or helpers. Or just close your eyes. Ask the element of earth to show you an experience you've had with earth. Once you have the memory you like, think of it as a story. Write it down if you wish: beginning, middle, and end. Then tell it out loud.

If I were to tell a story about earth, I might talk about gardening with my father or having a panic attack in an underground cave once. Mario might remember going to caves in Washington state and thinking about his father who went down into the mines his whole working life. The Old Mermaids might talk about the time they made bricks out of earth and built their house.

What story do you have about earth or about dirt? You know the drill now: Find yourself an Earth Tale.

Magic

Sing a wordless song. If you can't do it freely in your house, go to an empty room and close the door. You can begin with the vowels if you're not certain how to start. Sing each one as if you were joyful. Then sing each one as if you are grieving. Then just let the sound come out and go through your entire body. No words, just beautiful sound.

Do you feel the change in your body as you do this? This is the magic of sound, of song. If you can, go outside and sing to a tree. No words, just sound. Or sing to the birds. The sky. The Sun. Everything in Nature loves a song, especially your song.

Gift

Sister Bridget Mermaid gifts you with poetry and music today.

Old Mermaid Suggestion

"Sing, dance, create. If you have to choose, do all three at once."

—*Sister Bridget Mermaid*

Recipe

Love and Connection with a Tree

- One you
- One tree or bush or plant

Stand before the Tree and ask if it would like you to sing to it. You don't have to do this out loud if you're worried about someone seeing you talking to a tree. You probably won't hear a yes or a no, but you'll get a feeling if the Tree is open to it or not. As long as you don't feel anything strong that warns you off, open your mouth and begin a wordless song. Try to let go of any self-consciousness. After a second or a minute or whatever time, you will feel your chest open. Or something similar. That is your connection to the world and possibly to the tree. Keep singing until you feel finished.

All the Old Mermaids sang. Sisters Faye and Bridget Mermaid often created songs or chants especially for the desert plants and the critters.

One day, Sister Bridget Mermaid came upon a sparrow in the wash. It didn't fly away as she neared. In fact, it didn't move except for tilting its head now and again and looking stunned, the way a bird looks when it doesn't fly away. Sister Bridget Mermaid crouched in the sand near it. If it didn't fly away soon, some other creature was going to come by and eat it. If Sister Bridget Mermaid picked it up, she could harm it even more.

She began to softly sing. It was a lovely wordless song. She went through the vowels twice, and the bird cocked its head every time she sang, "Eh," so she sang it again and then again, playing with it, sometimes louder, sometimes softer. Until the bird seemed to yawn. Then it shivered, flapped its wings, and flew away.

Sister Bridget Mermaid smiled, stood, and then continued on her walk. When she told the story to the Old Mermaids later, Grand Mother Yemaya Mermaid said, "Sometimes it takes so much to heal the world, and sometimes it takes so little."

Sister Bridget Mermaid continued to sing to the world, and I hope you will, too.

Poetry by Mario Milosevic

If a Tree Sings in the Woods

Wind over limbs
is the melody,
trembling leaves
the lyrics.
Concerts occur
serendipitously
whenever the air
is restless
and your ear
is near.

Action

Do something creative. Sing a song, draw a picture, take a photo, cook a meal. Do something creative that is unusual for you.

And a Little Herstory

Sister Bridget Mermaid is named after the great Celtic triple goddess Brigid (pronounced "breed"). Brigid was part of the Tuatha Dé Danaan, and she was the goddess of healing, smithcraft, and poetry. It is said she invented whistling—to call your friends to you—and keening when she mourned the death of her son.

Day Nine
Day of the Saguaro

December 28

The Saguaro only grows in the Sonoran desert. This cactus is used by animals and humans for food, medicine, and shelter. The Tohono O'odham still harvest the fruit of the Saguaro in ways they have employed for hundreds of years. According to the National Parks Service, "The Tohono O'odham people have a complex, interdependent relationship with the Saguaro. It has a cosmological foundation that includes the saguaro once being human, a feature which the Tohono O'odham still recognize today."

Mario and I have about 22 saguaros on our property. We consider them our neighbors and guardians of our property. Most of them are young'uns, less than fifty years old most likely, judging from their lack of arms. They don't grow arms until they are at least 50 years old; some sources say it's actually 75-100 years before they get arms.

Saguaros seem so tough and present. Strong. They thrive in the Sonoran desert. This is a tough place to thrive.

When my father had heart surgery many years ago, I imagined the spirit of the Saguaro helping him stay here and "grow" strong. My father survived the surgery—a difficult and harrowing procedure. He lived more than a decade longer, far more than was expected. I think my papa had more than just a little saguaro in him.

The Old Mermaids definitely see the saguaros as people. Whenever they encounter one, they wave and call out a greeting.

Dreams

Have you dreamed of cacti or trees lately? Have they shown up at night for you? If not, daydream about your favorite tree or cactus. Have a conversation with it.

Ground and Center

When you do the Healing Roots Meditation, let your roots find the roots of plants and loosely intertwine with them now and again to say hello. Seek out a saguaro. Except for one tap root that goes down a couple of feet, saguaro roots are fairly shallow and travel laterally several feet. In any case, say hello and then let go and carry on to the center of the Earth.

Look for Guides and Signs

You know what to do. Is the Sky asking you to look up? Is the Wind whispering your name? Is that tree offering to shelter you should you need it? Signs can come from anything. On the side of a truck. In graffiti on the wall. In the shape of the twig in the dirt. It is just your way of connecting with the whole wide world and having a conversation. It doesn't have to be profound, but it is almost always fun and wow-inducing.

Magic

Protective Pouch

If you have a small empty pouch, you may use that. If not, make one. Find a piece of material in a color you like. It can be nice material or it can be from a clean rag. It's going to be in your pocket most of the time, so it doesn't need to be fancy. Cut out a circle anywhere from 4-6 inches in diameter. If you have cloth ribbon, cut off a piece 4-6 inches long. If you don't have ribbon, just cut a narrow piece from the same material as the circle. Make sure whatever you use is clean. If it's been used by someone else or as something else, you can purify it. Either literally clean it and/or sprinkle salt on it or set it on rose quartz for a bit and imagine it being cleansed for you.

Get a dried bean or three. Most any kind of bean will do. Not only can beans apparently stop quarreling, but in bygone times, it was believed they could ward off evil sorcerers: In other words, they are good for protection. You might sprinkle a bit of cinnamon on the beans or cut a sprig of rosemary from your garden; they both smell nice, and they're good protective herbs.

Take all of this to your quiet place along with some salt. Sit with the cloth and beans in front of you. Ask your guides to create a protective circle around you. Ground and center. Imagine you are safe and protected as you put the beans in the center of the cloth. Then close up the cloth around the beans so that you can tie the ribbon around the cloth just above the beans inside. As you wrap the ribbon around and then tie it, you can say some version of an old Irish charm of protection:

> Charm against arrow,
> Charm against sword,

Charm against spears,
Charm against any harm that comes my way.
In the name of the Maiden, Mother, and Crone.

Blow on the pouch. Sprinkle a little salt over it. Then put it in your pocket or purse. Every time you touch it or see it, you'll be reminded that you are protected.

Gift

Sister Sheila Na Giggles Mermaid's gift to you is "Guts!"

Old Mermaid Suggestion

"Get the starfish outta your eyes, sister."

—*Sister Sheila Na Giggles Mermaid*

Recipe

Sister Sheila Na Giggles Favorite: Charmed Moon Water Tea

Fill a clean jar with water. Put a lid on it, and set it outside under a bright Moon somewhere the creatures of the night won't find it. It doesn't have to be a full Moon, but that would be nice. If the water will freeze, then don't put it outside. Place it on a window sill where moonlight streams in. Ask the Moon to fill the water with good news of the world. Or fill the water with healing. Or peace. Whatever you like.

In the morning, decant the Charmed Moon Water into your

tea or coffee—or drink it straight. Charmed Moon Water is a wonderful tonic first thing in the morning.

Poetry by Mario Milosevic

Saguaro Shelter

Out on the trail,
as the horizon
was rising
to meet the sun,
a saguaro,
gilded in pure gold,
leaned close to me
and asked
if I was lost.
I raised my arm
in greeting
and thanked the saguaro
for its concern
and said I was fine.

We stood for a time
until we were both cloaked
in evening twilight,
neither of us willing
to pierce the serenity
that had grown up
around us.

Action

Speak the truth. Even though it may be difficult, speak the truth this day—and every day if you can.

And a Little Herstory

Sister Sheila Na Giggles Mermaid was named after Sheela-na-Gig. You've probably seen depictions of her in rock carvings over entrances in some Christian churches in Europe. She usually has a big head and face, and her bony hands have opened her vagina wide. She is often skeletal with big breasts, too.

Scholars don't really know who or what she is. Some say she is definitely Christian. Others claim she is a great Celtic goddess—womb to the tomb great goddess—put above Christian churches by the Celts to demonstrate their allegiance to their own gods. Although it is generally believed that she is a Pagan figure, according to the amazing scholar Patricia Monaghan, no one knows for certain. In modern times, Sheela-na-Gig has become a kind of feminist icon. However she is portrayed artistically, one cannot mistake her power or her attitude. She demonstrates the power of women over creation: womb to tomb.

I think of her as a trickster. For one thing, no one can credibly tell her story or history. For another, I want to laugh every time I see her. She reminds me of Baubo, only more fierce. Sister Sheila Na Giggles Mermaid is fierce, too, and she's a trickster. She understands reality—womb to tomb—just like her namesake.

Day Ten

Day of the Queen of the Night

December 29

One of the favorite plants of the Old Mermaids is the Queen of the Night. It only blooms one night a year. For the rest of the time, it looks like a dead stick in the ground.

The name Queen of the Night is actually an umbrella moniker for several cacti in the Cereus family. It is easy to miss the Queen of the Night because the plant looks so inconspicuous until it blooms (at night), and then the blossoms only last for a short time. The name cereus means "torch," and the flower can look like the light of a torch in the desert landscape.

Of course, Sister Magdelene Mermaid adored this plant almost best of all. She adored it before she knew about the blossom. When she first came upon one in the desert, she thought it was a plant that was about to die—or one that had died. But she let it be. She said to it, "Oh, you are a beauty. I know you are. You are queen of the cactus. You are deep and mysterious, I know this to be true."

Every time she came upon this plant, she would greet it and encourage it again, as it stood there like a stick under an old mesquite tree. Then one evening in June, Sissy Maggie was coming home late from dancing at Flat Rock Woman. She had somehow gotten separated from the others, and the Moon had not quite crested the Mountains yet. Sissy Maggie did not know where she was.

She called out, but nothing answered her, not even the coyotes. No owl. No blinking star. She was not afraid, but she was wary. She was still a newbie to the desert. What should she do next? She needed to get her bearings. She could still see the shadow of the mountains to the east so she knew she should probably keep going straight—north. But how straight? Didn't the path curve?

Just then, she spotted a white flower to her left. It seemed so bright, almost as if a star had fallen to the Earth. She moved closer to it and recognized it as the plant she had been encouraging for so many months. Only now, the stick was wearing a beautiful white flower.

"Ahhh," Sissy Maggie said. "You are surely the Queen of the Night. Thank you for your light."

Sister Magdelene Mermaid continued down the path, veering slightly to the left. As she walked another white blossom appeared on another stick that she had not noticed before. And then another and another, all showing her the way to the Old Mermaids Sanctuary.

Once she got home, Sissy Maggie told the other Old Mermaids about the Queen of the Night, and they all went out into the desert to ooh and ahh over the blossoms and to thank the Queens for helping Sissy Maggie find home again.

Dreams

You are deep into Yuletide, deep into the winter. Yet the days are growing longer and the nights shorter. How are your dreams? Are they more vivid, now, less vivid? Are you remembering more or less? Have you dreamed of flowers or blooming at night? Is there something in your life that you love but seems dead? What could you do to help it blossom again? Daydream and see if you can learn anything new about it.

Ground and Center

As you do the Healing Roots Meditation, remember to have your roots go all the way to the center of the Earth. Realize that your place is here and now, in this world.

Look for Guides and Signs

I bet you're getting good at this. Who is your guide for the day? Or have you had the same one for the whole time? Is there a sign out there for you? Today I want you to look for signs of spring that are just for you. Do you see a flower in an unexpected place? If so, it's a reminder to you that nothing lasts forever, even the bad times.

Ceremony

Find an object in your house that you once loved but you're not sure you care about any more. Take it to your quiet place. Sit while holding it or place it in front of you. Ask your guide or guides to make a safe circle around you.

Look at your object. Touch it. Remember it.

Does it still move you, speak to you, touch you? Truly?

If so, acknowledge it. And say something like, "Thank you for coming into my life. I will try to notice you more."

If it is no longer meaningful to you, release it. Imagine your index fingers and middle fingers as scissors. Imagine strings all around the object that are connected to you and cut those with your imaginary scissor fingers as you say something like, "It is so; I am letting you go. It is so; I am letting you go. It is done, under the Sun."

When you are finished, open the circle. If you're keeping the object, put it wherever you like. If you are done with the object, give it away, gift it, or recycle it.

You can do this with a bunch of objects at once, by the way, especially if you have trouble letting go of things. Everything in the world needs to be useful at some level. Hoarding or keeping things longer than you need them isn't good for anything. Love objects and let them go, as Sissy Maggie would say.

Magic

Change your mind about something today. Changing our minds about long-held beliefs can be the most powerful magic in the world. Starhawk defines magic as "changing consciousness at will." So how do you do that today? Maybe you've always said you don't like olives. What if you try an olive today and you actually like it? How cool would that be?

Or maybe someone will ask you about the designated hitter rule in baseball today. You've always hated it, but you think, well, maybe it's OK.

Try exploring something you've believed all your life to see if it's actually true. It is so startling and free to change one's mind: It is magic.

A few years ago, I drove back and forth from our home in the Columbia River Gorge to Seattle once a month for a year while taking classes at Antioch University to get a certificate in Permaculture and Sustainable Food Systems. It was always a horrible and dangerous drive that often left me sick, cranky, and completely stressed. Everything pushed my buttons.

I often stayed at the Quaker traveller's apartment for those weekends. It was a chilly basement room with two windows. Through one during the day, I could watch a huge male rat walking to and fro. Through the other I usually just saw pavement. I often had trouble falling asleep when I was there which made me crankier.

One night, light spilled through the parking lot window as I tried to sleep. Two people began chattering loudly. At first, I was angry. How dare they be so inconsiderate? Then I remembered when I was an 18-year-old backpacking through Europe. If I had been staying in a room in Paris, say, and a light came on and people started talking, it wouldn't have bothered me one bit. I would have enjoyed it as part of the experience of travelling. And wasn't that what I was? I was a stranger, a traveller to the Quaker house and Seattle. These people talking with the light on was just part of the experience. Immediately, my irritation disappeared. *I had changed my mind.* I was transformed. The situation was transformed. Pure magic. Soon after, the people left, the light went out, and I fell asleep.

Try it. Change your mind. You'll see. It will be magic.

Gift

Sister Magdelene Mermaid and all the Old Mermaids gift you with love.

Old Mermaid Suggestion

"You ask me to tell you about love. Showing is so much better."

—*Sister Magdelene Mermaid*

Recipe

Old Mermaids' Oatmeal

Prepare oatmeal as usual. Maybe this morning, you'll use some of your Charmed Moon Water for the liquid.

As it's cooking, you may want to ask for protection and good health and/or just a great day. Sprinkle in a little cinnamon for love and protection.

When the oatmeal is ready, pile on sliced bananas, whatever nuts you have on hand, pieces of apple, and blueberries. Maybe pour on a bit of maple syrup. Use milk, almond milk, or eat it without any "milk," which is what we do. Use whatever fixin's you have on hand: That is what makes it Old Mermaids' Oatmeal.

Poetry by Mario Milosevic

Guiding Light

Queen of the Night
we see you
drinking in the brilliance
of the moon.
You are full of light
and your true wild self.
We celebrate
your untamed night,
your brief blazing display,
and your constancy
in our imaginations.

Action

Sissy Maggie encourages you to "accept some sugar from the Universe."

And a Little Herstory

Sister Magdelene Mermaid was named after Mary Magdalen in her aspect as Mary, Mother goddess, and as the Mary Magdalen in the Gospel of Mary where she was the "bearer of secret knowledge," as Patricia Monaghan notes in her *Encyclopedia of Goddesses and Heroines.* I also think of Sister Magdelene Mermaid as Aphrodite, the very sensual goddess of the eastern Mediterranean long before she supposedly rose up from the sea in the foam of Uranus's semen.

Day Eleven
Day of the Owl

December 30

The owl has always been part of the story of the Old Mermaids, just as this place we now call the Old Mermaids Sanctuary has been part of their story. When we first started coming to the land we now call the Old Mermaids Sanctuary for our winter writing retreats, a great horned owl took up residence in the palm tree near where we slept. Nearly every night and morning, we would hear the owl coming or going. For us, this was a profound gift.

To have this mysterious wild thing so close was amazing. Of course the owl showed up in *Church of the Old Mermaids* very early on.

The owl represents different things in different cultures. To some, she is an omen of something wicked this way comes—or just an omen. To others, she is a symbol of wisdom and a companion to the goddess Athena or Minerva.

The owl is prodigious at being invisible. I have stared straight at an owl in a tree and not seen it until someone pointed it out. Even then I had to keep looking until suddenly I saw it. The owl here on the Sanctuary can be in the pine tree for hours, and I just can't spot it—until I do. Sometimes I think they are one of those creatures who stays invisible until it doesn't mind being seen.

Today you might want to try using your abilities in unseen ways. Or if you always feel invisible, use your abilities in visible ways.

Dreams

Have you dreamed of any wildlife lately? Last night, maybe? If not, pick a wild critter to daydream. Perhaps you want to have a conversation with an owl. Or a rabbit, a tree, a lizard? You choose and see what happens.

Ground and Center

Continue whatever method you are using to ground and center: the Healing Roots Meditation, the Merging Mountain Meditation, or your own method. Now that you have been doing it every morning for 10 days or more, have you noticed a difference?

Look for Guides and Signs

Today especially, see if any wildlife crosses your path. If so, interpret it like a dream. What would the dream creature mean to you or what would you mean to it if you showed up in their dream?

Ceremony

Honoring the Wild Things

To your altar or sacred space, add pictures of animals torn from magazines, animal cards, or any items you have that represent wild animals. Or create a place just for them somewhere in your living space. Some years I pull out all my animal collections and put them on the table along with gems and pieces of colored cloth.

As you create a place, imagine that wild animals are safe from harm, particularly human harm caused by pollution, habitat degradation, or hunting. Say a chant if you like. Make up your own or redo a healing chant you know. You can use this one if you like. It's a chant I wrote in Santa Fe that I have incorporated into healing sessions for years. I've rewritten it slightly to be used when wishing the wild animals the best. Say it three times.

Oh, wild ones. Hear this song.
This is how my will is done.
Every day under the Sun.
Every night under Stars and Moon
I am healer and the Wild Ones are healed.
Everywhere they go is haven.
Every place they stay is home.
These words dissolve
Disease, pain, and sickness.
Gone for now and ever more.
This is how my will is done.
Every day under the Sun.
Every night under Stars.
I am healer and the Wild Ones are healed.

When you take down the altar or sacred space after the 13 Days of Yuletide have concluded, you can say this chant again three times.

Magic

As you prepare for the next year, think again about the great magic of changing your mind. I wrote about this yesterday. Is there something you've been stubborn about? Some belief that has been with you since childhood that you can now release? I am not talking about your true core values. Did you read some things on the internet that you haven't truly investigated but you just "instinctively" believe? Be willing to find the truth especially if it will prove you wrong.

Gift

Sister Bea Wilder Mermaid gifts you with ecstatic dance.

Old Mermaid Suggestion

"Things change. Get over it."

—*Sister Bea Wilder Mermaid*

Old Mermaid Tale

Sister Bea Wilder and the Owl

One full Moon evening, Sister Bea Wilder Mermaid set off in the wash in search of jackrabbits dancing in the light of the full Moon. She had heard from the Old Neighbors that the jackrabbits do this regularly, even though Sister Bea had not found anyone who had actually witnessed it. She didn't really think she would find the jackrabbits dancing in the moonlight, but she hadn't been feeling herself lately. She couldn't figure out who she was in this new world and how she fit into the routine of every day life. She did not feel at home today or most days.

It was a little chilly since it was winter, so she had bundled up in a bright red coat Sissy Maggie had made for her. She wore a hat, scarf, and gloves that Sister DeeDee Lightful Mermaid had knit for her. Those had lots of holes in them, left by Sister DeeDee Lightful so that the "light could get in here and there."

The full Moon light was so bright that it was nearly as light out as daylight only so vastly different that Sister Bea Wilder Mermaid couldn't think of the words to describe the difference even to herself. Walking in the moonlight was like walking in a dream, only brighter and more real, she supposed, now that she had started dreaming.

Suddenly a shadow fell across her, and Sister Bea Wilder Mermaid looked up just in time to see a great horned owl fly overhead. She hadn't heard the bird's wings flap because the owl's wings were silent. The owl landed in the Y of a snag of a long dead mesquite tree and stared at Sister Bea Wilder Mermaid who stopped walking and stared right back.

The owl's eyes shined in the moonlight like two perfect silver coins.

It hooted, "Who, who?"

Sister Bea Wilder Mermaid nodded and said, "Are you asking yourself or are you asking me? Because if you're asking me who I am, I am Sister Bea Wilder Mermaid. At your service. If you're really asking who I am deep down, I guess I don't know. Although why would an owl ask me about my deepest truths? I don't actually think I have a deeper truth. I just am what I am. How about you? Who are you? Who?"

The owl blinked. And then it said, "I hadn't thought about it before. I was just trying to start a conversation."

"You succeeded," Sister Bea Wilder Mermaid said.

"With another owl," it said. "I wanted to start a conversation with another owl."

"Ahhh," Sister Bea Wilder Mermaid said. "I am not an owl. At least, not yet. Do you want to give me any hints on how to become one?"

"Again," the owl said, "I really haven't given this much thought. But perhaps asking the same insistent question over and over is a start. Wait. I hear someone calling out that question in the distance. Who, who, what a hoot. It might be my one true love."

Sister Bea Wilder Mermaid laughed. "You weren't really trying to start a conversation. You were looking for love."

The owl shrugged. "What is an identity crisis compared with love?"

It opened its giant wings and took off in the direction of the Moon or the sound of the owl's true love.

Sister Bea Wilder Mermaid stood quietly for a minute. What was an identity crisis compared to love? She sighed deeply. She loved being under this full Moon with her feet pressed firmly in the sand. She loved the owl. She loved the stars above. She loved their home and her sister mermaids. She grinned. She was starting to think like Sister Magdelene Mermaid.

She turned around and began running down the wash toward home. A bunny rabbit ran beside her, up out of the wash, for a while. Then a coyote replaced the rabbit. And then a stag. Along came a mountain lion. Then a bear. Sister Bea Wilder Mermaid laughed as she ran.

Just then she reached the house where Sister Ursula Divine Mermaid flung open the door and leaned out.

"There you are," Sister Laughs a Lot Mermaid said as she came to the door to stand next to Sister Ursula Divine Mermaid.

"We've been waiting for you," Sister Faye Mermaid said. "The wild times can't start without you."

"Who is it?" Grand Mother Yemaya Mermaid called from inside the house.

"It's me. Sister Bea Wilder Mermaid," she said. "I'm home."

Poetry by Mario Milosevic

Tree Soul, Owl Spirit

Through the day
the owl on its branch
gathers the tree's urge
for travel.
As dusk darkens the world,
the owl takes to the air
on silent spirited feathers,
carrying the soul
of the tree with it.
Adventurous pair,
they rise to expansive heights.
They are rootless

but grateful for the wind
through their leaves,
the light of the stars
guiding their eyes.

Action

If it is safe, go out into nature, even if it's just your backyard. Go there and dance. If it's too cold or just not conducive to such things, stay inside and dance. Recognize your true ecstatic self.

And a Little Herstory

Sister Bea Wilder Mermaid was easy to name. I love the word "bewilder." I always think it is pronounced incorrectly because we should be wilder. Sister Bea Wilder Mermaid encompasses all the Nature goddesses, including Artemis, of course. Every culture has a Nature deity, and Sister Bea Wilder Mermaid would be comfortable with all of them. And all of us could be a little wilder, don't you think? It's not about chaos and things out of control. Nature whole and healthy is balanced, and things flow easily. That is what being wilder truly means: going with the Natural flow.

Day Twelve
Day of the Dragonfly

December 31

In China, the dragonfly is a symbol of harmony, peace, and prosperity. To the Hopi and Pueblo people, the dragonfly was apparently a medicine creature, called upon by medicine people when a healing was needed. It was taboo to kill a dragonfly. To the Irish, the dragonfly symbolized transformation and perhaps a bit of illusion, since it was said fairies rode the dragonflies as though they were dragons or horses.

Here at the Sanctuary, we see lots of dragonflies dipping into our pool, perhaps mistaking it for a pond where they can drop their eggs. The Old Mermaids were charmed by the dragonflies. Everyone was in awe of their beauty and apparent fearlessness. After the Old Mermaids had to leave the Sanctuary, years or months or eons ago, it was rumored that one or more of them turned themselves into a dragonfly and flew away, never to return. The Old Neighbors said that was just a bad fairy tale: because if the Old Mermaids had to leave the Old Em Sanctuary, they wouldn't fly: They would swim away.

Dreams

The New Year is almost here. You can leave behind the last year. For good or ill, it is gone. In many ways, it is an artificial marking of time. Nothing suddenly changes once it is January 1st. However, perhaps you are more ready now for what is to come. You are more grounded. You are more in touch with your nature and Nature. How are your dreams? What did you dream last night? Draw it, if you can. No one else has to see it. Don't worry that you can or can't draw. Just get the crayons or colored pencils or just the blue pen you have on hand and draw what you saw and/or what you felt about it.

Ground and Center

Ahhh! It's almost here. Look what you've done. You've grounded and centered yourself since December 20, or at least some days between then and now. Do it again. Go deep into the Earth. This is your home. You belong here.

Look for Guides and Signs

Here. This is your sign for the day: YOU BELONG.

It doesn't have to be your only sign. Go and enjoy the day.

Ceremony

Find a piece or two of light-colored cloth. Get a pair of scissors, some paper, and a pen, one that will write on cloth and paper. Take this all to your quiet place. Ask your guide or guides to make a safe circle for you. Close your eyes. Think about all that you want to leave behind this year. Imagine it all going away. When your mind is clear of what you want to leave behind, imagine what you would like to bring into your life for the new year.

When you feel done with that process, open your eyes and

write down the list of wishes for the New Year for yourself. Be general and be specific.

After you've made your wishes, you may make wishes for others only if they are not specific. For instance, you can wish for health and happiness for everyone you know. But don't wish for your sister Kate to get a divorce. If someone has asked you to pray for them about a particular issue, then you have their permission to write a wish for them. Otherwise, this is about what you want.

Then cut or tear narrow pieces of cloth about a foot long and two inches wide. On each of these pieces of cloth, write one wish each for the new year. Think about what you want as you write it. After you finish with each one, blow on it, and say something like, "May this wish come to be, with harm to none not even me."

Put the cloth wishes in a pile. When you're finished, go outside and hang them on a nearby tree, your balcony, or along the fence. Find something where you live that will hold onto the cloth while the wind carries your wishes to the appropriate sources. If you're tying them to a living thing like a tree, make certain the tree is OK with it. Weeks or months later, take the wishes down and dispose of them, confident that some or all of your wishes will come true.

Magic

We will most likely have good times and bad times this coming year. We have experience to carry us through, no matter the times. Beauty always exists along with horror in the world. The magic is not turning away from what is real. The magic is knowing that you do not know everything and never will. The magic is that we can find some beauty in the world almost always without having to pretend that horror doesn't exist. Magic is creating even during uncertain times, and creation can consist of making a sandwich, drawing a stick figure, or creating a good time with another person.

Gift

The Old Mermaids gift you with healing and magic.

Old Mermaid Suggestion

"The rest is . . . mystery."

—*Sister Faye Mermaid*

Recipe

For a Good Year

Prepare to face the year, whatever it may bring. Use all that you've learned here and all that you've learned through your life to get you here. Stay connected to the Earth, her creatures, and yourself. You are here and now. Even if you don't feel as though you were made for these times, you were made during these times. Stay in conversation with the world. Now and again, find stillness and grace amidst it all. Give yourself permission to be happy, sad, angry, joyful. You carry the stuff of stars in you, and the stars carry you.

Old Mermaid Tale

Together: Part One

Every year and sometimes more than once a year, sometimes on Hallow's Eve, or sometimes around Solstice, the Old Mermaids walked to a river to greet the new year or a new beginning, whichever came first. They lived in the desert so finding a moving body of water was sometimes an adventure in itself. Many of the Old Neighbors came with them. The Old Ems relied on their knowledge of the land, on Grand Mother Yemaya's ability to smell water, and on Sister Faye Mermaid's ability to hear the songs of the river. This meant they almost always found running water.

It was quite a sight to see the Old Mermaids and some of the Old Neighbors streaming across the desert like their own kind of flood, dressed in colorful clothes with small rocks weighing down their pockets. They talked and laughed, told stories and jokes, and sang now and again.

On this particular year, they found a stream coming out of an ancient spring, up in Serenity Canyon where Saguaro people saluted them every few feet. Old cottonwoods, ash, and willow trees hung over the water and shaded the trail, making the desert winter day almost cool. They found the deepest part of the water.

Then several of them stood on the edge of the river and took out a stone or rock from their pockets and held it up and said something like, "I am letting go of all the pain I had this year," or "I'm releasing my anger about Charlie dying," or "I'm letting go of poverty," and then they would toss the stone into the flowing water. Everyone near them would say, "May it be so."

Not everyone said what they were releasing out loud. Sometimes they would just toss the stone into the water and watch the ripples. But the bystanders still said, "May it be so."

Everyone always liked to hear what the Old Mermaids had to say.

One year Sister Sheila Na Giggles Mermaid said, "Let go of that song in my head that the bumblebee left me last week. It is driving me a little crazy."

"May it be so," the others responded.

Sister Ruby Rosarita Mermaid once said, "I want to let go of that large piece of cinnamon that does not taste quite right. I could throw it away, but if it's just my taste buds, then I release the bad taste of cinnamon."

"May it be so," they said.

Sister Magdelene Mermaid said, "I want to let go of the bad feelings I engendered between me and that doe over by Laughing Woman Springs. I talked to her babies without checking with her first, and she has not liked me since."

"May it be so."

You get the idea. It was fun to see what they said each year. On this particular year, Grand Mother Yemaya Mermaid said, "I want to release the world from sickness, sadness, and war."

"May it be so," everyone said, and then they cheered and clapped.

After everyone had their says at the river's edge, it was time for the gifting.

But that's a story for another day . . . like tomorrow.

Poetry by Mario Milosevic

A Flame of Dragonflies

Darting like
winged needles
weaving heat
into the fabric
of the wind.
Tongues of fire
flickering the air.
You follow an
erratic path,
leaving us
earthbound
and lonely.
Surely you follow
a well-worn

celestial path
to paradise?
Or perhaps
nothing more
than the long
unspooling
of a lonely
torch song.

Action

Sister Faye Mermaid encourages you to create magic today.

And a Little Herstory

Sister Faye Mermaid was named after Morgan Le Faye, of course. So much has been written about Morgan Le Faye, especially regarding her relationship with Arthur. What is more intriguing to me is that she was probably another goddess figure that was diminished when Christianity became predominant. We just don't know enough about her yet.

Barbara Walker calls her a "Celtic death-goddess: Morgan the Fate, or Fata Morgana, or the Triple Morrigan . . . Sometimes she was a Ninefold Goddess." Walker also says that Morgan Le

Faye and the other morgans or sea-women could become mermaids, and they had glorious palaces at the bottom of the sea.

Her name seems to indicate she is part of the faery realms (Le Fay/Faye). I see her as a powerful magician, the ultimate witch who knows the chants and spells and isn't afraid to step into the energy rivers and pull out magic and power.

Day Thirteen
Day of the Desert Tortoise

January 1

Happy New Year! You made it through one year and into another. You did it through luck, perseverance, and pluck. Maybe along with some tears. You were made for these times, even if it doesn't always feel like it.

The desert tortoise is especially made for difficult times. Its biology enables it to tolerate imbalances in water, energy, and salt on a daily basis. It can easily protect itself from most of the dangers of the world by pulling in its head and limbs.

The tortoise is slow, but it wins the race.

Here at the Old Mermaids Sanctuary, a one-eyed desert tortoise visited last year. We think we figured out from the shape of his shell that he was a male. One of our barometer bushes was blooming purple then. One-eyed Jack stayed near that bush munching on purple blossoms until he was ready to move on. We wish he would return to us for a visit, but it's possible he's here, and we just don't see him. The tortoises live most of the time underground.

The Old Mermaids encountered the desert tortoise now and again. The tortoises were out and about a bit more those days. They would cross the wash one by one, sometimes with their little ones sliding in the sand behind them. The Old Mermaids would nod or tip their hats and let the turtles be on their way. Whatever they were doing, it wasn't any of the Old Ems' business.

Some of the Old Neighbors believed that the desert tortoises knew all the secrets of the New Desert, just like the whales knew all the secrets of the Old Sea. The tales told about such things warned against ever directly asking the turtles for this knowledge because then they would never tell you. You had to wait patiently and just see: Maybe one day they would tell you a secret and maybe one day they wouldn't. It was said that the more you knew about the land where you lived and walked and worked, the more likely the desert tortoise would stop and tell you a thing or two. So the Old Mermaids never asked a tortoise a single question, yet the rumor is they learned quite a lot of turtle wisdom.

You might try this approach. Maybe not with a desert tortoise if you don't live in the desert. Try it with any wild thing. Have patience. Learn. And wait and see.

Dreams

What are dreams? Dreams are very personal. I encourage you not to look at dream books to figure out the meaning of your dreams, at least not unless you are completely stumped. Symbols in dreams are highly personal. They're based on our experiences and what family and culture we come from.

For instance when I dream of a snake, I most often feel as though I've been visited by the goddess. It's a beautiful dream. If my mother had a snake dream, she would have awakened terrified because she was terrified of snakes. That said, a few days ago, I dreamed that I was surrounded by rattlesnakes in the water, and they were trying to get to me. I had this dream soon after I wrote this particular part of the 13 Days. It's a reminder to me that dream snake visits are not always pleasant. I did not feel as though I was visited by any deity. I felt quite rattled by the dream, no pun intended.

None of this answers the original question: What are dreams? That answer varies depending upon the culture. For the Old Mermaids, they did not start dreaming until they came to the New Desert, so they believed most of their dreams were messages from their ancestors and the Old Sea.

Dreaming time is considered sacred space in most cultures. For the ancient Egyptians, dreams were a way to communicate with the dead. The Hawaiians practiced "soul sleep" as a way to communicate with their ancestral guardians. Some Tibetan Buddhists practice dream yoga which (very simply put) is a kind of lucid dreaming.

For the Japanese, the first dream of the New Year—*hatsuyume*—can foretell your luck in the coming year. It is especially auspicious if you dream of Mount Fuji, a hawk, or an eggplant. So what was your hatsuyume? I would encourage you not to be stressed if you had a bad dream last night. Unless you are Japanese or were raised in a Japanese culture, your dreaming life is probably not attuned to having a hatsuyume.

My guess is that you already have your own beliefs about what dreams are to you. I'm not certain what dreams are. Some cultures believe we are living another life in our dreams, that it's a completely other reality, and sometimes I think that is the case with my dreaming.

Sometimes I have what feels like big dreams with big wisdom, but I don't always get what that wisdom is. Sometimes dreams feel like great moving art pieces or a memory of the life I lead while I'm asleep.

I now think of dreams as gifts and don't stress over them. I like remembering them, and often I do find a message in them, whether it is intended by my higher self or the Universe or not.

No one knows for certain what dreams are or how they

come into being, not even scientists. My advice is to use them for good, for wisdom, whatever they are. So much of our life and our quality of life comes down to how we interpret absolutely everything in our lives, including our dreams.

Ground and Center

Today is the first day of the New Year. If you have been doing the grounding and centering work for the last 13 days, I know that you've noticed some benefits. Now you can decide how you want to accomplish this same kind of centering for the coming year. Keep doing the Healing Roots Meditation, do the Merging Mountain Meditation now and again, and/or find a new centering method. Just keep it up. You can always put down roots no matter the situation.

Look for Guides and Signs

You have had guides or a guide for the last twelve days. If this was new to you, did you enjoy it? Do you want to go forward co-creating with your guide? If you've been looking for signs, did you enjoy it?

I observe Nature all the time and try to figure out what I can learn about the environment from these "signs." I ask if the drought is affecting the trees, bushes, flowers yet. Do I need to intervene in any way and if so how? I try to assess my responsibility literally: what is my ability to respond to these signs from Nature?

My advice is to look for signs if it's fun, and incorporate a guide into your everyday living as long as it's an equal relationship. You may need advice now and again, but it's your life. Don't let any being try to dominate it, human or otherwise.

That said, today is a great time to do a little divination. I encourage you to try it the Old Mermaids Way if you haven't already. This means we don't look at these tools as a way to tell the future but as tips to inspire us to go forward, or see the reading as a message from the Ancestors. Mostly have fun. Today is not a day for doom and gloom. Today is a day for celebrating the real possibility of healing and joy.

Ceremony

Gifted

The first of the year is a great time to do a Gifted ceremony for yourself or others. See the Old Mermaids Tale for today for some ideas of what to do. In a way it's the simple act of re-gifting yourself since you've had these gifts your whole life.

Think of some gifts you would like for the year, gifts that you may have always had but gifts you want to revitalize this year: gifts of good health, prosperity, love, more time in Nature. Things like that. Write a few on pieces of paper. Put them in a bowl or a cup. Dress up or dress down. Prepare food for afterward or don't. Make it as simple or as elaborate as you like. When you want to begin, take a piece of paper out of the bowl and read the gift out loud by saying something like, "I gift myself with good health this year and beyond." Or whatever the gift is. Close your eyes and feel that gift seeping into every cell in your body. Breathe with it. Then go onto the next piece of paper. Or if you feel finished, then be finished. Celebrate. You've been Gifted!

Magic

We've done some practical magic during these 13 days, some kitchen witchery, and some steps toward great magic: changing our minds and truly transforming. You get to decide what you would like to do going forward.

Remember my dream of the Rumanian woman who told me we must always thank the spirits of everything? So I do that. Thanking everything and being in a state of gratitude does no harm. What if our attention to that which we don't know or understand can awaken true magic in ourselves and the world? We need to remember we know so little. That doesn't mean turning away from science or reason. In fact, we must embrace science. We must embrace logic as we connect with Nature and explore the world.

It is good to know how to research and learn to discern the truth. It is good to understand that we don't know everything, and we will never know everything. As Iris DeMent sang, "I think I'll just let the mystery be."

One can be rational and reasonable and believe in science and still talk to birds, trees, possible faeries, and all the Ancestors. For one thing, it just feels polite and neighborly.

Gift

Mother Star Stupendous Mermaid and all the Old Ems gift you with the Stars, Earth, Moon, and Sun.

Old Mermaid Suggestion

"All the wisdom of the ages can be distilled into one suggestion: Be."

—Mother Star Stupendous Mermaid

Recipe

Bring on the Love

Take a clean glass jar and fill it halfway with water. If the weather is good, take it outside. If not, stay indoors. Have the lid nearby and hold the jar in one or two hands.

Breathe and imagine everything you love in the world whole and healthy. Try to imagine those critters you adore safe and thriving. Imagine the people in your life safe and healthy and thriving. Imagine yourself healthy and thriving. Let yourself fill up with love. Let go of any feelings of loss, if you can. If you can't, save this for another time. When you are all filled up with love, exhale into the jar and then put the lid on. Shake the jar. After you shake it, open it and drink it down. Your belly is now filled up with love. Nothing better, eh?

Old Mermaid Tale

Together: Part Two

After the Old Neighbors and the Old Mermaids let their troubles stream away from them, it was time for the Gifted Ceremony.

The Old Mermaids chose a large stone that rested in the winter Sun near the creek as the seat for the gifting. The Old Neighbors took turns sitting by the water and receiving their gifts. In the ash tree above, a black-throated sparrow or two watched.

The Old Mermaids came to the Old Neighbors one by one to bestow their gifts. Mother Star Stupendous Mermaid sometimes sprinkled stardust on the Old Neighbor before saying something like, "I gift you with the mysteries of the Universe."

Sister Sophia Mermaid said, "I gift you with interesting conversations."

Sissy Maggie Mermaid often brought the sparkling gold and red fairy wand that FeyMay had given her the last time the faery came through the rift. Sissy Maggie tapped the shoulders of the Old Neighbor she was blessing and said, "I gift you with all the love you need and want."

Sister Ruby Rosarita Mermaid said, "I gift you with the most delicious soups you've ever had," or "I gift you with nourishment."

Sister Ursula Divine Mermaid said something like, "I gift you with healing self-knowledge," or "I gift you with dance," or "I gift you with a happy life."

Sister Bea Wilder Mermaid might say something like, "I gift you with joy and happiness."

All the Old Mermaids gifted all the Old Neighbors, and

then, usually as a group, the Old Neighbors surrounded the Old Ems and shouted out gifts to them. "I gift you with plenty of cake!" "We gift you with laughter." "I gift you with interesting friends."

The Old Neighbors gifted each other, too. The gifting went on and on until they were finished. Then they ate and drank and talked while standing near the edge of the creek. When it was time, they all walked home, filled with the promises of the new year.

May it be so for you, too.

Happy New Year, everyone!

Poetry by Mario Milosevic

Turtle Dreams

They step slowly
into the new year.
Long-lived,
they've seen many beginnings
and are sturdy guides
to commencements.
No hurry here.
The world will
always be set out
before them:
a lush banquet
congruent with

their own sensibilities.
The world on their backs
holding the promise
of amazing things
to come.

Action

Meditate. Have a good year. May you be blessed and gifted all the days of the year.

And a Little Herstory

Mother Star Stupendous Mermaid was named after the ancient Near East goddess Astarte. Like most goddesses after the patriarchy came into existence, her true origin story is difficult to piece together. It's possible Astarte could be another name for Atargatis, the original mermaid goddess. She may be a version of Ishtar and/or Aphrodite. But I actually named Mother Star Stupendous Mermaid after Astarte because I liked the "star" in her name (even though that's not what her name means). Simple as that.

About the Author

Kim Antieau's books include many accounts of the Old Mermaids and their adventures in the Old Sea and the New Desert. Among them are *Church of the Old Mermaids, The Fish Wife,* and *The Blue Tail.* She has also distilled much of the wisdom of the Old Mermaids into several non-fiction books, including *The Old Mermaids Mystery School, The Old Mermaids Book of Days and Nights* and *The Old Mermaids Oracle.* Kim has also created a divination deck of cards, *The Old Mermaids Wisdom Cards.* Her other books include *The Jigsaw Woman, Whackadoodle Times, Ruby's Imagine, Queendom: Feast of the Saints, The Monster's Daughter, Killing Beauty, Coyote Cowgirl, The Salmon Mysteries,* and *Answering the Creative Call.* She lives in the Southwest with her husband, Mario Milosevic.

More about Kim's writing at her website: kimantieau.com.

Kim's photographs at kimantieau.smugmug.com.

www.ingramcontent.com/pod-product-compliance
Lightning Source LLC
Chambersburg PA
CBHW081740100526
44592CB00015B/2243